Soul Healing with Our Animal Companions

"Tammy Billups teaches us that we aren't in it alone. The powerful connection we have with our animals can fulfill them and us in ways we never knew. *Soul Healing with Our Animal Companions* helps us all make that realization in a wonderfully engaging read that will encourage everyone to learn the unspoken signals of their furry friends in order to nourish a deeper and meaningful animal-human relationship."

MIKE BETTES, METEOROLOGIST AT THE WEATHER CHANNEL
AND COMPANION TO JOPLYN, THE ORPHANED DOG HE RESCUED
DURING THE 2011 JOPLIN, MISSOURI, TORNADO

"*Soul Healing with Our Animal Companions* gives us a comprehensive avenue to help connect with our animals at a deep level. Tammy's true stories with her heart-centered presentation easily explain animals' roles in our lives. She offers simple solutions to turn things around through self-discovery and the unconditional love we share with our animal companions. If you have concerns about your animal or just love them dearly, this is a must-read!"

CAROL KOMITOR,
FOUNDER OF HEALING TOUCH FOR ANIMALS®

"Tammy calls us to examine our all-too-human extremes of mistreatment and neglect of animals versus our codependent and overattentive neediness with our animal companions to find a healthier higher ground. She gently yet firmly teaches us to look for the divine purpose and deeper meaning in all our predicaments with our animals as reflections of ourselves. *Soul Healing with Our Animal Companions* is an essential read for all animal lovers, whether you are on the front lines of animal activism or quietly living with animal beloveds. It will open you, empower you, deepen you, and work magic on your own soul."

ANYAA T. MCANDREW, M.A., L.P.C., N.C.C.,
TRANSPERSONAL SHAMANIC PSYCHOTHERAPIST

"*Soul Healing with Our Animal Companions* gives the reader a more conscious understanding of the relationship between humans and their pets. This book shows how animals mirror our own lives and emotions and gift us endless blessings that many times we completely miss. By understanding how we are in relationship with our pets, we can more quickly help them to feel better. My wish is for all people to have exposure to the vast knowledge and teachings of *Soul Healing with Our Animal Companions* for their own healing and the well-being of their pets. Thanks, Tammy, for sharing your knowledge, guidance, and gifts with us!"

GIGI GRAVES, FOUNDER AND EXECUTIVE DIRECTOR
OF OUR PAL'S PLACE, INC.

"*Soul Healing with Our Animal Companions'* ultimate message is one of greater spiritual consciousness and personal evolution. By recognizing that our beloved pets are in our lives because we call to them, and vice versa, we can expedite our growth as well as that of our pets."

PAUL CHEN, *NATURAL AWAKENINGS* MAGAZINE

"Pet lovers know there is a unique connection between human and pet. It's only when we go deeper into animal and human psychology that we see just how unique that connection truly is. Animal healer Tammy Billups takes us beyond the fur—the obvious affection for our pets—and shows us our connection is heart to heart and soul to soul. Written in an easy, entertaining, and enlightening style, *Soul Healing with Our Animal Companions* dives deep with real life anecdotes to illuminate behavioral patterns and how they were successfully overcome. . . . a must-read for any animal lover who wishes to deepen the connection with their pet and discover and heal behavioral issues for a happy and healthy home."

DON REED SIMMONS, VISIONARY BUSINESS CONSULTANT AND
SHAMANIC TEACHER AND PRACTITIONER

Soul Healing
with
Our Animal Companions

The Hidden Keys to a
**Deeper Animal-Human
Connection**

Tammy Billups

Bear & Company
Rochester, Vermont • Toronto, Canada

Bear & Company
One Park Street
Rochester, Vermont 05767
www.BearandCompanyBooks.com

Text stock is SFI certified

Bear & Company is a division of Inner Traditions International

Library of Congress Cataloging-in-Publication Data
Names: Billups, Tammy, author.
Title: Soul healing with our animal companions : the hidden keys to a deeper animal-human connection / Tammy Billups.
Other titles: Beyond the fur
Description: [Second edition]. | Rochester, Vermont : Bear & Company, [2018] | "Originally published in 2016 by Booklogix under the title Beyond the Fur: Discover the Hidden Keys to Understanding Your Animals' Behaviors and Physical Issues." | Includes index.
Identifiers: LCCN 2017034549 (print) | LCCN 2017060183 (e-book) | ISBN 9781591433057 (paperback) | ISBN 9781591433064 (e-book)
Subjects: LCSH: Human-animal relationships—Psychological aspects. | Pet Owners—Psychology. | Pets—Behavior.
Classification: LCC QL85 .B53 2018 (print) | LCC QL85 (e-book) | DDC 591.5—dc23
LC record available at https://lccn.loc.gov/2017034549

Printed and bound in the United States by Lake book Manufacturing, Inc. The text stock is SFI certified. The Sustainable Forestry Initiative® program promotes sustainable forest management.

10 9 8 7 6 5 4 3 2 1

Text design by Priscilla Baker and layout by Debbie Glogover
This book was typeset in Garamond Premier Pro with Bodoni Std and ITC Avant Garde Gothic used as display typefaces

To send correspondence to the author of this book, mail a first-class letter to the author c/o Inner Traditions • Bear & Company, One Park Street, Rochester, VT 05767, and we will forward the communication, or contact the author directly at **www.tammybillups.com**.

This book is for all animal lovers wanting to bring
more awareness and light into the heart of their relationships
with their animal companions in the name of love.

For Khalua,
the first soul to teach me
about unconditional love.

Khalua
1988–2000

When all is said and done, we're all just walking each other home.

RAM DASS

Contents

A Letter
to the Reader

Dear Animal Lover,

Thank you for choosing to read *Soul Healing with Our Animal Companions*. It has been my dream for many years to write about the findings of my work with both people and animals. I am excited to share this information with you so you can better recognize and understand your animals' deeper teachings just waiting to be revealed.

You are their guardians, but they are your teachers. Their teachings have an underlying purpose, to allow in more love and more joy into both of your lives.

This book talks a lot about how animals serve you and your family, but I know that if you were drawn to this book, the animals that you have helped, rescued, and shared your home and heart with are better for having had you in their lives. They would not have grown and healed and loved as deeply if you hadn't cared for them as you did.

I'm a big believer in the power of stating intentions and affirming them formally. So I want to share with you my firm beliefs and purpose for writing this book:

1. To help people everywhere unlock the potential of a deeper, more conscious relationship with their animals, for the benefit of them both;

2. To empower people to trust themselves about decisions they may have to make on behalf of their animal companions;

3. To help people understand their animals and their teachings so that the more difficult times can be easier, and the easier times can be even better, and;

4. To create more love and less suffering in the hearts of animals and the people who love them.

I hope you will think of this book as your morning cup of java for your relationships with all of the animals in your life. It will wake you up to seeing your animals more clearly and give you even more reason to love and appreciate their presence in your life.

May you always feel love in your heart, peace in your soul, and the joy of sharing your life with animals.

With love,

Tammy

Personal
Acknowledgments

I would like to express my gratitude to the many people who gave their time, love, and funds to support my dream of seeing this book come to fruition. Their wonderful energy is in every word and on every page—right alongside mine.

Thank you to my extraordinary friends for your steadfast belief in this project. I am especially grateful to Tara and Helen, who were my extra-loving set of eyes. They read every word and gave their invaluable insights and feedback, all in the name of friendship. To Cynthia, for your divinely guided nudges, please accept my deep gratitude. To Hope and Nanette, your selfless gifts were immeasurable. To Gigi, thank you for sharing your heart and your experiences with me to better help others.

Thank you to my number one cheerleader, my sister Shelley. I love you more than you'll ever know.

I'm grateful to every animal that has graced my journey, for they have helped me immensely to grow, love, and, in turn, to serve them.

For believing in my dream, I humbly thank those who

supported my original campaign to self-publish this book.

Each client I've been blessed to work with has also been my teacher, and I send heartfelt gratitude to each one. I also thank those who gave permission to share their stories so that others might learn from them and be helped.

While writing, my mantra was "I allow the Divine to express through me." This served to remind me of the higher purpose of the words that were flowing through my heart to the pages of this book.

Thank you, God, for always having my back, and for your ability to get through to my heart no matter the situation. I am so very grateful to consciously be on this journey together.

Gratitude for Animal Rescuers

I would like to thank every person who has ever helped to rescue an animal and/or provide a healing environment for them in which they may feel loved and safe. Those who choose to foster and rescue an animal may find themselves on an emotional roller coaster. They are seemingly driven by a higher purpose, and their willingness to help animals—while knowing their hearts could be broken time and time again—is both admirable and courageous.

If you are one of these people, please take a moment to breathe in gratitude from every animal you have ever rescued or helped to move forward to a loving "forever home." You have made such a positive difference in their lives. I humbly thank you for your service to the animal kingdom.

Opening to Love

What was happening to me was too horrific to focus on, so I moved my attention only a few yards away where a cat was struggling in the arms of a man who was about to throw her into a raging fire in an old, outdoor metal trashcan. It wasn't the first time I'd witnessed a cat losing its life at the hands of these same men.

As a young child, it is a natural reaction to instinctively "check out" when something traumatic is being experienced or perceived. Sadly, I'd become accustomed to disconnecting from all of the pain, abuse, and invasiveness happening around and to me.

But that particular night was different. While watching this beautiful cat in her final moments, she suddenly turned to look directly at me, and we locked eyes. This jolted me back into the present moment. Both of us were helpless to alter our circumstances, and yet somehow our eyes found each other, and then . . . *I felt her. I actually felt what she was feeling and thinking.* We were not only relating to each other; I could feel our energetic connection as if we were one—heart-to-heart and soul-to-soul. I had never felt more intimately connected to another being in my entire life.

Oddly, there was great comfort in this moment for me as a child when the cat and I were one, because I could feel that she was at peace in her soul with what was about to happen. I remember wanting to go with her, but that was not meant to be.

That moment was the first time I can remember being able to energetically connect to another soul and know their feelings and thoughts. However, I repressed that ability—or gift—until the year I turned forty.

Most of us remember certain birthdays more than others. Like a lot of people, my turning forty was not an occasion I welcomed. What I didn't realize then was that the universe was going to pull the rug—or my life as I knew it—out from under me that year. I would repeatedly be brought to my knees in heartbreaking anguish. This would force me to question every thought and belief I'd had up until that point.

My mother's final chapter of life a few months after this milestone birthday prompted me to begin opening my mind to what happens after we die. This was in part due to the fact that my mother talked openly about conversations she was having with friends and family who had already passed. They were coming around her to ease her transition to the other side. This was very convincing proof of the soul continuing its journey, which brought me great comfort, but also made me want to know more about our souls' journey.

At that time in my life, I was sharing my home and life with my three cats who were more like children to me. Weeks after returning home from my mom's memorial service, my calico kitty, Khalua, passed away from colon cancer. Her transition was actually more difficult for me to handle than my mother's was because Khalua had been my first experience of receiving unconditional love.

Suddenly, the day after Khalua's transition, I was able to

see energy all around me, everywhere. In that energy, I could see my mother, Khalua, and numerous other beings that I didn't know and didn't *want* to know. I was—amazingly—seeing their souls. I was in uncharted territory without a compass. The experience felt incredibly invasive, and I was terrified. I no longer had any privacy because this wasn't anything like a television, which I could just turn off.

Even more upsetting, memories of awful events from my childhood that I had repressed were simultaneously unlocked, like someone who had amnesia suddenly remembering everything. Ideally, people have gone through some type of therapy or healing to begin to develop the inner resources and self-parenting skills necessary to better deal with unlocking the fear and emotional pain of traumatic childhood memories. I had not. I felt broken open at my core, and the endless, raw pain and sleepless nights that I began to endure were unbearable, as emotions were released that had been buried for decades.

Memories of abuse from many different men surfaced, in addition to my mother's shocking role in much of it. There were also many memories from my childhood, of watching animals heartlessly being abused. I'm certain this is now why I've been so drawn to doing all I can to help and serve them in my life and healing practice.

Only months after Khalua passed away, my other two cats, Vasi and Bailey, joined her in heaven at the young ages of six and eight. It's easy now to look back and recognize that all three of my cats left that year because their job was to help me get to that point—and no further. They'd been emotionally supporting me in endless ways—ways in which I hope my animals will never have to support me again.

Like many before me going through a difficult life-changing period, I wondered when and if my painful experiences would ever end. It took me a while to get to the "perks" part of having a zero-to-sixty spiritual awakening filled with so many losses. As I searched for help and an understanding of everything I was going through, I eventually was led to a licensed professional counselor, who was also a gifted energy practitioner and teacher. My inner healing journey helped me transform my body, mind, and soul so much that I no longer needed the many daily medications I thought I'd be on for the rest of my life. This whole process proved to be the most amazing journey of finding myself—one that most people will never stand in line to buy a ticket for.

With the release of each layer of protection around my heart, I came to know gratitude and the spiritual bliss that comes with feeling and being connected to all there is—to God, to nature, and to other souls. It was through my personal healing journey and interface therapy certification training that I learned how to interpret what I was feeling, seeing, and sensing energetically. Surely my "enhanced vision" had happened to me for a reason! At this time, I enthusiastically embraced my true life purpose and opened a practice to help all beings enhance and change their lives through this extraordinary holistic modality of releasing emotional wounds energetically so that the body can do what it knows how to do best: heal itself.

It was indeed the worst year of my life, but it was also the best, for it catapulted me into a new way of living and being, filled with love and with the rewarding work that I've been blessed to do for the last seventeen years. Every experience, the good ones as well as the not-so-good ones, helped to create the woman I am today, wherein I am able to share my learnings on behalf of both animals and people, so that they may allow more love into their lives.

PART ONE
THE ORIGIN

How is it that animals understand things I do not know, but it is certain that they do understand. Perhaps there is a language which is not made of words and everything in the world understands it. Perhaps there is a soul hidden in everything and it can always speak, without even making a sound, to another soul.

FRANCES HODGSON BURNETT

1

My Pathway
to Animals

Given that I've worked with animals all these years, most people assume I grew up surrounded by a menagerie of animals who were my childhood buddies. Unfortunately, I did not. My mother was raised to be a clean freak and a heavy-handed disciplinarian, and the one dog Dad brought home for us when I was in fifth grade did not fare well at her hands. Snoopy was rehomed to a farm where I hope and pray he was able to discharge the toxic energy that one year spent living in our home no doubt engendered.

Once out on my own, I moved and traveled a fair amount with my career. Thus, adopting a cat seemed to be the perfect antidote to fulfilling my desire for furry companionship. Although I quickly found out that I was highly allergic to cats, I had become smitten with the unconditional love of my first kitten, Khalua, so much so that I chose to get weekly allergy shots rather than rehome my beloved pet.

Over the following years, my family grew to three wonderful felines that I fell head over heels in love with. It would be fair to say that their every need was taken care of with my utmost care and attention.

My Catharsis

As I mention in the introduction to this book, a few months after my fortieth birthday, my mother died. Her death occurred six weeks after she'd found out she had melanoma. Weeks after my mother's memorial service, my beloved Khalua joined her on the other side. It wasn't long after Khalua transitioned that my other two cats, Bailey and Vasi, passed away as well. It was a very difficult time for me, but through that period, I awakened to an entirely new way of looking at life. I'd been stuck in the "money will buy me happiness" lifestyle up to that point, which, I might add, had not been working. I quickly got a reality check in what was important to me, and, newsflash, it wasn't the next promotion.

In the middle of all of these losses, I was devastated, and feeling raw and endless pain, so I sought out healing help. As it turned out, the counselor I gravitated toward was also an energy therapist, and although I had no idea what that meant at the time, I was open to trying anything that might help me. Immediately after the session, I felt amazingly better. It was unbelievable! I recall thinking that I couldn't remember ever feeling that good before. While still sitting on her practitioner table after that first session, I told her with utmost clarity, "I want to do what you do." After many months of regularly receiving energy sessions and releasing a lot of pain and grief, I enthusiastically signed up for an extensive training program to become certified in the trade so I could begin helping other people heal as well.

While in training on how to help people heal by clearing past traumas and emotional wounds held in their energy fields, I began wondering how animals would respond to the same healing process. During my training time at the Center for Integrative Therapy, I learned in-depth about the five emotional core wounds that people have and how they show up in one's energy field, actions, and behavior. They may even reveal themselves as physical issues.

Some of My Early Findings

When I first began facilitating energy healing sessions on my friends' animals, I found it fascinating to discover that they carry the same energetic patterns and emotional wounding as people do. However, my search to discover more about how these patterns and wounds manifest within animals came up empty. Although I did find a couple of other very good animal energy healing training programs that enhanced my knowledge base (Healing Touch for Animals® and Silvia Hartmann's Energy Healing for Animals program), ultimately it was my years of training to work on people that would contribute the most to my effectiveness in working with animals.

I did quickly learn, however, that when I was working with animals they were frequently sponges of their people's emotions—conscious and unconscious—and mirrored them in many ways. Animals choose to live with people so that they can heal the same issues together—not separately. When I realized this, the importance of my working with both animals and people—to the benefit of both—became abundantly clear to me.

The positive results of the early animal sessions I facilitated awakened me to the relevance of this holistic healing modality. I found that energy healing sessions were even more productive with animals because animals don't overthink or question the validity of the work like their two-legged guardians do. They simply trust and relax into the session with a clear knowing that the energy healing process is a natural one.

> *Animals choose to live with people*
> *so that they can heal the same issues*
> *together—not separately.*

Given that there's no such thing as a placebo effect in an animal, the results shared by people who saw immediate and positive changes in their pets were very credible. And there were also many extraordinary healings and positive outcomes I *couldn't* explain. One of my early clients had been told by her veterinarian that her horse Maxie would never be able to run again because she had developed osteochondritis dissecans in her leg. After two sessions, Maxie was running—an outcome that left the vet scratching his head.

By simply understanding your animals' messages by better interpreting their ailments and behaviors, there can be immediate and positive shifts for you both. I really *get* the dynamics of how our animals mirror us, for every animal in my life has been a divine messenger that arrived with many teachings, of which I have been an avid student.

I want to help you be one too.

Essential Wisdom

There is so much more to the relationships you have with your animals than meets the eye. Anyone who has opened their heart to an animal knows the bond goes beyond what is said and done. There is an unspoken connection—a *knowing* between the two of you.

Over the years I've come to realize through my work with people and animals that the soul connection we have with them shows up in a multitude of ways. Many times they're trying to communicate with us, but their messages go under the radar or undercover. This is because our awareness, or level of consciousness, isn't up to speed about how to best interpret the communication coming our way.

As children we're drawn to animals because of the acceptance and love we receive from them. Animals won't give us a chore to do, tell us we're bad, or, worse, abuse us. They are there for us when we are down, seemingly seeing inside us and knowing exactly what we need, when we need it. At the same time, they gift us with the freedom of being our completely authentic selves. We then let them in and love them with our whole hearts because we trust them—with them we feel completely safe.

In time, as the relationship of trust and awareness develops, they become our teachers as well as our most devoted companions.

2

Energy and Emotions

Animal lovers all agree that animals have feelings. They feel love, pain, joy, sadness, fear, and even grief. Compared to many people, animals live more from the right side of their brain, so they are more easily connected to their intuition and the energetic flow of divine love. When divine love is flowing through an animal or a person, life is just plain easier. It's more peaceful, healthy, fun, loving, and safe.

Everything is Energy

All beings have an energy field around and through them. We are all energetic beings having a physical experience. Every *thing* also has an energetic vibration to it, with love being on the highest end of the scale and fear on the opposite end.

We are all energetic beings having a physical experience.

Emotions are held in the energy field, and repressed emotions and unhealed emotional wounds create congestion, or blocks, in the energy field. Physical ailments, pain, and even negative behaviors are the result of having congested energy. So taking good care of your animals' energy fields is vital to the overall health of their bodies and to ensure that physical issues don't develop.

How your animals feel is reflected in its energy field. If they're feeling good, their energy will be bright, expansive, and carry a high vibration. If they're sick or depressed, their energy field will contract and be congested, even murky. Energy is something everyone senses at some level. You might just have a feeling something is off with your animal. That's your intuition kicking in. The two of you are so intimately connected that you'll both naturally sense the other's energy. Animals feel all of the changes, stress, and imbalances of their people and the household that they live in. Depending on how much exercise they get, as well as their age, diet, and unhealed emotional wounds, they can feel anxious or depressed, or even have similar health issues that stress causes in their human companions.

The good news is that animals are tuned into energy in ways that most people are not and will instinctively know when they need to have a meditative rest to clear their energy. The not so good news is that the closer animals are to their people emotionally, the more likely they are to absorb their energy, which can make it more difficult for the animals to clear their own. Because your animal is more likely to absorb the emotions you are pushing down and not expressing, it's important for you to be proactive in releasing your emotions in a healthy way. Understanding more about the connection between your emotions, your energy, and your health can be a game changer for your well-being as well as the well-being of your animals. A congested energy field can affect all aspects of one's emotional, physical, and spiritual health. Consequently, this knowledge can significantly influence the choices you make about your animals' care. Knowing how sensitive they are to your emotions is also motivation for you to do your own energetic housekeeping.

Adding meditation to your daily routine is a great place to start—it's a powerful generator of energetic well-being. Meditation activates and restores balance to your pineal gland. When your pineal gland is fully functioning, you will be better able to sense and feel energy, given that your natural intuition will be restored.

Introducing new ways of thinking and healing to your belief system takes courage, because people aren't typically excited about making changes in their lifestyle. I honor you for embracing new, more progressive ways of creating health and well-being for you and your animals.

Healing Animals with Energy

There are many unknowns about how and why energy healing actually works. We can be in our left brain all day long, trying to figure it out, but it probably won't do us much good. The process of trusting it requires faith in not knowing all of the details and instead tapping into your feelings. Receiving energy healing sessions myself allowed my body to heal in ways that mainstream protocols couldn't begin to touch. The bottom line for me was that my body healed, and I no longer needed to take the numerous medications I'd been on. That was enough of a result for me.

I've seen the same reaction in my clients and my own animals. That doesn't mean they've never visited the vet. It simply means that energy healing, or bioenergetics, has been a very powerful alternative that has helped them tremendously.

Animals are extremely receptive to this work, and healing through the energy field just happens to come with the fringe benefits of being noninvasive and not having any negative side effects.

When a trained energy facilitator connects to an animal's energy field with permission and with positive intention, the energy naturally flows where the healer's attention goes. Think of a time when you wanted your pet to come and sit with you and they instantaneously arrived at your side without you having called them out loud. That's not a coincidence; it's because of your energetic connection. The process is similar when an energy practitioner focuses in on their client. Where intention goes, energy flows.

During a session, your animal's energy field is naturally being restored and rebalanced while simultaneously getting grounded in Mother Earth. When a trained practitioner is facilitating a session, he or she intentionally connects with the universal flow of energy and becomes a conduit for the highest and best healing to occur. Predictably, in every session the higher vibrational, yummy emotions like love, compassion, and joy will backfill the void left when lower vibrational, fear-based emotional energy is released.

Most animals will simply sink into a peaceful surrender position during the session, indicating their trust in the experience. Often you may see them releasing deep sighs as they expel energy, and/or stretch ever so gently to reposition themselves as they feel the energy moving through them. Again, this gentle healing method will help them release any energetic disturbances, toxins, or emotional congestion they are carrying. Once the animal's energy has been cleared, its body is healthier, and this state will induce and promote natural healing to unfold.

There are many energy healing modalities and techniques available that different practitioners are trained in and use when working with animals. None is better or worse than any other. It's important to know, though, that the clearer, more grounded the practitioner is, the more productive the animal's sessions will be.

Essential Wisdom

Healing emotional wounds with energy healing, or bioenergetics, is not a new healing phenomenon. Many people are aware of how this holistic, noninvasive alternative healing modality has the ability to transform lives.

And I am one of those lives.

⁖————※————⁖

Be grateful for whoever comes, because each has been sent as a guide from the beyond.

RUMI

PART TWO

THE REFLECTION

The more you stop to observe and learn from animals, the healthier and more peaceful your life will be.

WAYNE DYER

3

The Looking Glass

While teaching a class called Kindness and Compassion for Animals to six- to eight-year-olds at a local no-kill animal center, I asked the children to tell me which dog they were most drawn to and why. Olivia, with a huge, enthusiastic smile on her face, was the first to raise her hand. She said with a giggle that the dog at the shelter she liked best was Harvey, because he was happy, fun, and liked to play a lot. When I called upon the quiet child in the back of the room, who was sitting by himself, he said the dog he was drawn to was Chloe because she just looked sad, like she needed a friend.

The Law of Attraction in Action

This was the law of attraction in its purest form: The young ones so easily expressed how they instinctively felt the unconscious pull of an animal that was energetically wired the same way they were. The truth is that you will always be attracted most to the animals that are like you in some way and have gifts to offer you for your growth.

Your pets might have similar physical qualities, behaviors,

and personalities as you. Or you might be attracted to animals that have the same emotional wounds that you do. There are many levels of attraction between you and your pets, and there are no mistakes about the animals who choose to share their lives with you, however brief the amount of time they spend with you might be.

What do you see when you look at your animal? Think about how you describe your pet to people. When I first began working with animals (and their people, because they go hand in hand), I couldn't help but notice that as they were describing their animals, they were frequently painting a picture of themselves.

The beauty you see in your animal companion is also in you. Every unconditional drop of love you see and feel from them is a big part of why you're together. They're mirroring your divine self so that you can know how wonderful you are at your core, and you can begin to reveal more of your inner light and pay it forward.

> *The beauty you see in your*
> *animal companion is also in you.*

Our animals will always reflect what we like or don't like in ourselves. I remember when my former husband would talk about our dog Toro, he would frequently describe him as stubborn and bullheaded. I, however, saw the beautiful lab as patient and kind. Same dog, different mirror.

The animal-human connection is magnetic, and you will unconsciously be drawn to the animals that mirror you and hold messages for healing, growth, and even karmic clearing for you both. It is a divinely orchestrated, symbiotic relationship that I believe is crucial to the healing of this planet, for it serves the admirable purpose of allowing more love into the hearts of people who might otherwise find it unsafe to allow in love from others.

Over the years, I've come to realize it's impossible *not* to talk about the mirroring and bigger picture of why your animal companions are in your life, because their messages are key to enhancing all of your relationships, especially the one you have with yourself. Think about how knowing, receiving, and acting on your pet's messages could enhance both of your lives! It's a life tool unlike any other and a gift you definitely need to unwrap and use every single day.

Animals have their own personalities, of course, but if they're in your life, however briefly, they are representing a part of you that you need to be exposed to for your personal growth. Maybe it's a part that needs healing, and maybe it's a beautiful part of yourself that you need to see and recognize in order to feel a deeper level of self-love. This I know for sure: The sooner their messages come into your awareness, the sooner you will both feel better and have more pleasurable interactions and experiences.

Your animals mirror you on different levels and in many ways. You might call the mirroring synchronicity or meaningful coincidences. But whatever you call this beautiful multidimensional reflection, it holds incredibly useful tools for you to receive, interpret, and utilize their soul messages, created especially for you.

If you let animals get emotionally close to you—maybe even closer than you let people get—then they are likely your best "Earth schoolteachers." You will greatly honor these teachers by raising your awareness, or consciousness, about the messages they are always giving you rather than focusing entirely on their physical world.

Physical Mirroring

Some people are subconsciously drawn to an animal that bears a resemblance to their physical appearance. These people are typically unaware of these similarities when the animal first comes into their life. This type of mirroring is the easiest to detect. More than anything else, it's interesting and fun to notice how often it happens. It may be the grumpy-looking man with the bulldog or the woman with the long red hair who has an Irish setter. Sometimes it's the shape of the head, the hairstyle, or a prominent nose we notice. Whatever it is, this type of mirroring happens frequently.

Then there is the fascinating phenomenon that occurs when you and your animal companion have similar physical ailments. If this has happened to you, you're not alone. It happens all the time—much more than you might realize. There are endless stories of people and their animals suffering similar injuries or ailments and moving forward to heal together, physically and emotionally.

When I was in my thirties, I had not yet begun my inner healing journey, and I was frequently sick. I had chronic sinus infections, allergies, asthma, gallstones and endometriosis which required many surgeries. I was on eight daily medications that I thought I'd be on for the rest of my life. Imagine my surprise when my cat Vasi developed asthma right after I was diagnosed with asthma! There would prove to be many other "coincidences" wherein my pets mirrored my health, ranging from urinary tract infections, colon problems, and skin issues. I dared not discuss my observations of the shared physical ailments with anyone back then. I thought people would assume I was nuts to even suggest that my animals were mirroring my exact physical issues.

Once I'd embraced a holistic healing journey, however, it became crystal clear to me that this mirroring was not a coincidence. As I energetically cleared my emotional wounds and trauma, my physical body healed, and I gradually got off all of my medications. Even better, my animals physically healed as well.

It is still and always will be nothing short of miraculous to me how healing our emotional wounds through the energetic field will set the stage for our bodies to heal themselves, just as they were designed to do. Talk about motivation to heal one's inner wounds! Like any animal lover, no way did I want my beloved animal companions carrying *my* physical issues. This truth will forever motivate me to continue to work on myself so that all the beings I love will not have to absorb my physical symptoms. My animals have always been phenomenal teachers, and I will be eternally grateful for their sacrifices so that I can help others learn how their animals are teachers and healers for them as well.

Soon after I began facilitating energy healing sessions on animals, I noticed it wasn't only *my* animals that mirrored and absorbed physical ailments from their respective guardian. During the debriefing of their animals' sessions, I began asking my clients if they could relate to anything that I'd observed and felt from their animals' energy and physical bodies. Here is an example of such an experience.

A Change in Behavior:
Charlie's Story

Carol called asking for help in identifying why her dog Charlie had changed his behavior, and she wondered if it had a physical cause. She'd taken him to her veterinarian and everything had checked out okay, but her sense was that something else was going on with him.

As soon as I connected with Charlie, I could feel a lot of excess congested energy in his hips and spine, and my feeling was that it was not his. Carol had only mentioned that he was more lethargic and acted like he wasn't feeling well, so I was surprised by what I felt and saw in his energy field. The amount of dense, lower-vibration energy he cleared during the session from his hips was incredible. After a good snooze to integrate the work from the session, Charlie was back to his old self. But what was interesting was that after his session, Carol shared with me that she'd recently had lower back surgery. Charlie was serving his mom and trying to help her feel better by absorbing her back pain issues.

Many times, maybe as often as 40 to 50 percent of the time, when I mention a particular area on the animal where I feel energetic congestion during a session, the person will inform me that they also have a physical issue in that part of their body. Frequently, your pets will be able to clear the energy they absorb from their surroundings before it manifests physically, as it had with Charlie. Other times the animal might have a more difficult time moving it out, and it could, in turn, manifest as physical symptoms that need attention and healing.

Animals love serving their people because they are evolving their soul as well. It is part of why they are with you. Because of this, it would behoove you to be proactive in your emotional health so there is less for your animal companions to mirror or absorb. Most of your physical issues are rooted in unhealed emotional wounds that, when cleared, can and will heal your physical ailments.

Some animals are more likely than others to absorb their person's emotional and physical manifestations. They may have experienced invasiveness in the past, which can cause weaker boundaries. Or, they are just generally more sensitive, or are master healers (more about them in Part Three of this book). Depending on many factors, they might need additional help by way of an energy healing modality to clear what they've absorbed.

> *Most of your physical issues are rooted in*
> *unhealed emotional wounds that, when cleared,*
> *can and will heal your physical ailments.*

Behavioral and Personality Mirroring

You can tell a lot about a person when you meet their animals. Are their animals friendly? Afraid? Hyper? Lazy? Scattered? Bossy? Animals will be happy to tell you the true personalities of their people if you observe their actions and behaviors. Maybe you've already noticed the similarities between members of your family or your friends and their animals. Now, perhaps, I've gotten you thinking about your animals and their personalities and how they match yours. Like it or not, they are mirroring a part of you. What you see in them is in you.

A great way to observe behavioral and personality mirroring at its best is to go to a dog park. It's better than people watching at the airport! You might just notice how the calmest man there has three serene, easygoing dogs. The loud guy has the dog that won't stop barking. The person acting like a bully has the aggressive pooch. The rigid-looking woman without a hair out of place probably has a perfect-looking dog that never misbehaves. The following is an example of pets who mirror their people.

Finding Peace:
Prince's Story

Rose called to get help for her little dog's behavior issues. I could barely make out what she was saying because she spoke so fast and loud and in such a scattered, jumbled way. She was all over the place and it was difficult to take in what she was talking about. I felt that she just needed to sit down, get grounded, and meditate for an hour.

But when her words had a chance to sink in, I finally understood what she was saying about Prince, her dog. Apparently, Prince had an annoying habit (her words) of constantly jumping up on her, and he wouldn't settle down. She said he was always frenetically busy, he constantly got on her last nerve, and she needed help so that he would be more peaceful.

They were both ungrounded and mirrored very overactive personalities. Given that Rose was unaware of the reflection her dog provided, she was actually personalizing his behavior and literally thought his actions were intended to make her crazy.

I conducted an energy healing session for Prince, during which time he became grounded and his energy field was cleared and lightened up considerably. Rose was thrilled with the results. Prince would go on to receive two more sessions, after which Rose said she'd never seen him so peaceful and calm. Prince held the grounding longer after each session, but then he'd revert back to the constant jumping and busy behavior again. This was due to the fact that Rose didn't simultaneously work on her own grounding and healing, as I'd gently recommended to her to do, for it would help Prince as well as her.

Instead, she discontinued the sessions.

If Rose had simultaneously started a meditation or yoga practice, walked each day, or received sessions herself, to name a few options, Prince would have greatly benefited, for he would have mirrored that behavior as well. It was clear that Rose and Prince were used to the feeling of being ungrounded, which probably felt normal or more comfortable to them, and so that's the level they chose to remain at.

People and animals become ungrounded due to fearful experiences and many times can continue all of their lives feeling unsafe and anxious. With intention and commitment, it can take a shorter amount of time than someone thinks to begin feeling more comfortable being grounded, safe, and peaceful.

There are endless gifts your animal companions are mirroring for you via their behaviors and personalities. Is your focus on something you see that you don't like about your pet? Then it might be time for you to look in the mirror of truth to explore what might need to be changed in terms of your own behavior. If you don't get it right the first time, no worries. Your animal will continue holding up the mirror until you see your behavior for what it really is and begin to take action that will manifest transformation that endures for the long haul.

As soon as you shift your behavior and heal the wound behind it, you will see a different mirror when you look at your animal. On the flip side, if you see something you like in your animal, that is in you as well. They may be mirroring it for you to recognize, believe in, and integrate so you can shine your inner light even brighter.

Unconscious Mirroring

Some of the most powerful messages come through unconscious mirroring with your animals. It is powerful from the respect that once you receive your message, there can be a positive and instantaneous shift for you both.

Animal lovers know that their beloved pets want to help them feel better, especially during hard times. Often I hear from clients that they don't want their animals to be around them when they cry or are upset so their companions won't be exposed to the emotions that are coming up to clear. People don't want to burden any beings they love and in those moments they can feel unworthy of *receiving* love, which contributes to the inclination to push their animals away. But it's more than that. Experienced animal lovers consciously or unconsciously know that their pets can and will absorb their emotions and want to protect them from this.

First, know that it doesn't matter how physically close you are to each other when you release your emotions. The two of you are so connected energetically that what *you* feel, your pet feels too, regardless of his or her physical proximity to you. Some animals are more likely than others to feel and absorb the emotions being released, depending on the deeper reasons you're in each other's lives.

By far, and I mean by a long shot, the emotions you repress and put under lock and key and don't want to deal with are much more likely to be mirrored by your animals in ways that, typically, you won't like seeing. Your repressed emotions are also more likely to negatively affect their quality of life. So releasing your emotions in healthy ways as they come up is a gift to you both; stuffing them down—not so much.

Examples of some healthy ways to release your emotions

include meditating, crying (as mentioned previously), 20-30 minutes of daily physical movement, indulging in hot Epsom salt baths, journaling, or utilizing the help of a healing practitioner or body worker for deeper emotional clearing.

The following are examples that illustrate how animals will mirror us so that we can adjust our behaviors as necessary.

Reflecting the Truth Within:
Sundance's Story

There was a period of time when my cat Sundance would sit on my desk directly in front of my computer monitor when I was working and incessantly meow as if she was mad about something. This would happen every single day! She would even raise it a few decibels when I was on an important business call, which did not sit well with me. I would close her out of my office, and even still she would sit at the door and meow. I was really frustrated and angry about this.

One day during my meditation time, I was thinking about her annoying habit, and a thought popped in my mind that I couldn't ignore. Suddenly, I had clarity that she was trying to tell me that I was pushing down anger—that I wasn't dealing with it. Once I got her real message and took some time to check in with myself regarding what I might be angry about, the situation became even clearer.

I had been repressing a lot of anger about my recruiting business, which back then I was conducting simultaneously with my healing practice. I had built-up anger about recruiting because I wanted to focus all of my time on my healing practice, but I didn't believe, from a financial standpoint, that I could let the recruiting work go. When I was sitting at my desk, I was forcing myself to do work that I no longer loved.

> Sundance was trying to tell me what was going on by helping me tap into the anger that longed to be acknowledged and released. When I realized this, I made time to do active healing and release work around the issue, apologized to Sundance, and expressed heartfelt gratitude for her insistence on helping me to heal.
>
> Once I became aware of her message, her behavior stopped. I mean it completely stopped, as in she has never done it again.

The first clue in determining what emotion you are repressing when you react to your animal's perceived negative behavior is to notice how their behavior is prompting you to feel. Once you do this, take the feeling inside to investigate where in your life you might have that same unexpressed emotion.

Sometimes your animal may exhibit a negative behavior. Simultaneous with this, you may be unconsciously projecting onto them the negative aspects of someone who has wronged you in the past. In that moment, they become the father who never listened to you or the older brother who pestered you. Thus, the sooner you are able to see the higher purpose of your animal's actions, the better off you'll both be. Directing more of the same negative emotion toward your animal when you are frustrated will simply fuel the fire for the same behavior to continue or even escalate. (We will explore this issue of projection more fully in Chapter Seven, "Projection Happens.")

Hidden Courage:
Jespurr's Story

Lisa was so excited when she brought home her handsome cat Jespurr. She couldn't wait for her friends to meet him. Much to Lisa's dismay, however, while Jespurr was very *interactive with her, whenever anyone else came into the house, he holed up under the bed. She'd try bringing him out so people could meet him and kept hoping he'd get more relaxed over time and be more social. He didn't. At this point she called me to see if energy healing could help him feel safer around other people.*

As I got to know Lisa by doing sessions on Jespurr, I learned that with a lot of preparation, there was a part of Lisa that could be very social, but her true nature was quite introverted, and she felt safest and most authentic when at home by herself. Lisa expressed that she'd never had the need or desire to have children, so she thought that getting a cat was a good idea.

Try as she might, however, while she cared about Jespurr, she remained detached from forming a deeper bond with him. I had the sense that she was disappointed with his personality and judged him for being an introvert. However, the deeper truth was that she judged and disliked the part of herself that Jespurr mirrored for her.

Over many years, Lisa, Jespurr, and I worked together from time to time clearing Jespurr's energy, and then I didn't hear from her. When next I caught up with Lisa, she shared that Jespurr had passed away months prior. As we spoke, I learned that Lisa had met and fallen in love with a man with two small children, and they were now living together and creating a new life with one another and the children.

Lisa sounded peaceful and happy about having a very different lifestyle at home. She'd gotten completely out of her comfort zone and felt safe enough to let this gentleman and his two children into her heart and into her life. The mirror that Jespurr had always held up for Lisa was no longer needed; that part of her had healed.

Reflections on Early Passing

I especially wanted to share Lisa's story with you because sometimes our animals leave us when we have integrated, healed, and learned what they have come to teach us. I've had this happen with animals that left earlier than I'd ever hoped or desired they would. Their jobs done, they were ready to go back home. In each of those situations, I'd gone through tremendous inner healing and shifts in my life.

Although losing a cherished pet may be tragic and painful, know that they would not transition without either your having healed something that they came to help you with, or that their transition is providing a gift or teaching for you. There is always a higher plan and purpose that arrives with every animal that graces your presence.

Essential Wisdom

The best way to strengthen your ability to receive your animals' messages is by making an intention to be open to allowing a deeper, more spiritual relationship with them, and to recognize that they are your mirror. They are willing hosts for your spiritual growth. Your animals are drawn to you like magnets to mirror what you are most needing to receive or release in any given moment.

4

Symbolic Messages

Your animals are amazing hosts and mirrors through which incredible wisdom, inspiration, and answers to your questions can arrive in many ways, including through the genius of symbolism. When you open your mind and set your intention to receive symbolic messages from your animals, the universe will deliver the goods. Symbolism can take your journey together to a whole new level. It will enhance your interconnection with the animal kingdom and all there is. The only requirement on your part is that you believe the messages when they show up on your doorstep and remain open to the possibilities that will assuredly present themselves to you.

There are so many examples I could share with you about these types of messages, but I'll narrow it down to those that I think will best give you some real food for thought as to what to specifically look for as you undertake this adventure of looking for the hidden gift, or purpose, in your animal's actions. When you begin to raise your awareness around receiving these types of messages, you'll also tap into yet another level of gratitude for your animal companions and the many ways and reasons they're in your life. Here is an example of that from my own life.

Believing:
MaiTai's Story

One day I was sitting on the sofa feeling sorry for myself about a work project that had just tanked. Then I noticed my cat MaiTai attempting to find a way to jump up on the top of the armoire, a place he'd never tried to reach before. Intently, I watched him. All the while, I was thinking there was no way he would be successful.

With the utmost determination, though, he zeroed in on his goal. However, every time he jumped, he missed and fell. And yet without ever taking his eye off of the top of the armoire, he figured out there was a chair on its other side that could offer him better leverage. Moving to that chair, he took one more leap and then bam! *He arrived at his destination! Then he just sat there—smug and proud—calmly grooming himself as if everything had gone down exactly as planned.*

He never even considered the option that he wouldn't reach his goal. He didn't back down and feel sorry for himself after a couple of tries and whine, "Oh, well, I guess it wasn't supposed to happen." He believed it was possible in every fiber of his being and quickly determined a route to success. As I reflected on what I had just witnessed, I realized there was a huge message for me of the utmost importance in his actions. MaiTai was telling me to keep trying and that there was more than one way to reach my goal; I needed to remain focused and not give up.

There was no coincidence in the timing of his trying to get on top of the armoire. It was exactly the message and inspiration I needed at that moment in time to look at things differently with the work project that I'd assumed was never going to come together. I did indeed come up with another way for the project to come to a positive resolution. More than that, I still reflect on that afternoon's sequence of events, which to this day, whenever I am faced with obstacles in my path, inspires me to take action, never give up, and always go after my dreams.

Here are some other amazing stories about how our animals are giving us messages through symbolism.

Seeing Beyond and Within:
Carter's Story

Jenny volunteered to foster Carter, a dog who had completely lost his sight. The veterinarian told her that surgery might help to restore his sight, but it was a long shot at best. Specifically, there was only a 10 percent chance the surgery would restore a very minimal amount of his vision. The animal rescue organization that had sheltered Carter decided to move forward with it anyway and was able to raise the funding for the surgery. I donated healing sessions to expedite Carter's recovery time post-surgery and hold space for any deeper healing that he might need.

The first time Carter even met Jenny was directly after his surgery. The plan was that he would go home with her—to be housed in a small room of her abode, a place he had never been before. He would have bandages over his eyes for two weeks, and Jenny would be his caretaker during his recovery. An orphan found on the streets who didn't trust people, Carter, without any sight, had to learn to rely on Jenny completely to get all of his needs met, while being in a completely foreign place (her home). Jenny was concerned about how he would react. Would he exhibit a fight-or-flight response to being in a small, contained room that he didn't know and couldn't see—or would he adapt and learn to trust her?

During my conversations with Jenny, it was clear that she was emotionally connecting with Carter on a deeper level. She would tell me with a heavy heart of his struggles after he'd first arrived at her house, and how fearful he was while learning the logistics of the room and a new routine. But then he started to learn that the easier and more courageous choice was to trust his kind and loving caretaker. Jenny observed his process with great admiration, for he was clearly letting go of long-standing fears about trust. During his energetic healing sessions with me, he released a lot of fear and began healing the emotional wounds of his past that had created his trust issues in the first place.

It was during Carter's second week with Jenny that she received a powerful healing message from him through the symbolism of his being blind and having trust issues. Jenny had been in the middle of trying to make a very difficult, gut-wrenching decision, and through Carter's teachings she realized she hadn't been trusting the process and was instead acting and reacting out of fear.

However, by watching Carter give up his fear and learn to trust, like a lightbulb going on, Jenny realized she had not been seeing her personal situation accurately. She then realized how she could look at her own situation differently and trust herself and her heart to make the right decision.

The entire two weeks were incredibly healing and life-changing for both Jenny and Carter. To this day, Jenny will still close her eyes to feel what she is not seeing with her physical eyes to remind her to trust—to trust God, the universe, and mostly herself.

At the end of the two weeks, Jenny took Carter in to get the bandages removed, and the vet was shocked and surprised to find that Carter's eyesight had been completely restored. He said it was a miracle. Indeed it was, for both Carter and Jenny were now seeing clearly. Every detail of their being together had been divinely orchestrated and the best possible outcome had been achieved for them both.

Every life experience arrives with the potential gift of inner transformation.

Balance:
K'en's Story

Rebecca called requesting a healing session for her cat K'en. When I asked her what was transpiring, she told me that K'en was suddenly refusing to walk on one of her legs. After having an in-depth exam and X-rays taken by K'en's veterinarian, it was still a mystery as to why she wouldn't put any weight on the leg. The vet determined that there wasn't any physical reason why K'en wasn't using her leg; she wasn't expressing any signs of pain or tenderness at all.

I proceeded to conduct an energy healing session on K'en. Afterward I felt guided to ask Rebecca if any part of her own life felt off-balance. In reply, she gasped as if she'd been blindsided. She wasn't expecting me to ask about her and certainly didn't expect me to ask a question that she resonated so much with. Yes, she told me, astonished. She'd been feeling very unbalanced in the prior weeks, in the arenas of her work and her marriage, and instead of improving, the situation was only getting worse.

After I suggested that K'en might be giving her a message to get back in balance, Rebecca realized that she could

no longer procrastinate dealing with and making some impor-
tant adjustments in her life. Immediately, she began making
better choices for herself and her family. Simultaneously,
K'en suddenly began walking normally again—in complete
balance.

Can you begin to see the power that comes from raising your awareness by looking for the symbolic interpretations of your animals' actions? Here's one more story from the school of symbolism from a dear friend.

Empowerment:
Yintu's Story

Lorelei arrived home one day and was surprised to hear her
cat, Yintu, meowing loudly as if upset and stuck somewhere,
but she couldn't locate him. Finally, she noticed he was stuck
high in a tree, directly above her. Yintu was clearly distressed
and calling out for help. Frozen with fear, he believed he
was unable to change his predicament on his own. Lorelei,
picking up on his fearful energy, believed she also did not
have the resources within herself to help him get down. She
frantically began calling friends and neighbors, but no one
was available to help.

Then it suddenly occurred to her that Yintu represented
a fearful inner child aspect of herself that had always felt
powerless to change her life's circumstances on her own.
Immediately, she ran back outside and began encouraging
him to climb down the tree. The fearful part of her persona
was also listening very closely to her words of encouragement
to the cat.

Over and over again, she enthusiastically said, "You can
do this, Yintu! You've got this! I know you have it within

you to get down on your own! I believe in you! You have the power within you to do this and more." Yintu, feeling and feeding off of Lorelei's strength and shift in energy and power, slowly began making his way down the tree until he successfully reached the ground.

Again, Yintu was symbolically representing a powerless inner-child aspect of Lorelei that was stuck and in need of some internal parenting to shift. Once Lorelei received the message, she was elated at the realization and the ensuing transformation was immediate for them both.

Essential Wisdom

Sometimes just the awareness of the higher purpose of your animals' actions brings an immediate shift in their behavior and/or physical issues. Think about something your animals have done in the past and what their teaching might have been for you and what they may be mirroring.

Look beyond the physical action to see if it might have anything to do with something that was going on in your life at that time, or is going on in your life now. If there is a connection, feel it. Embrace it. Let it be a gift that prompts change within you and take action accordingly for your highest good. That's what's needed for both you and your animal to feel better. The shift in energy allows for a win-win outcome.

The reality of your relationship with your animals is that you signed up for this ride together to help each other heal, through love and compassion, similar emotional wounds. Help your highest and best self—and theirs—emerge by utilizing the mirrors your animals reflect. *Always be sure to express your heartfelt gratitude to your companions, for they are working hard for you, helping you to wake up to a more authentic life, full of purpose and joy.*

Yintu

If we could read the minds of animals, we would find only truths.

ANTHONY DOUGLAS WILLIAMS

PART THREE

THE CONNECTION

You cannot share your life with a dog, as I had done in Bournemouth, or a cat, and not know perfectly well that animals have personalities and minds and feelings.

JANE GOODALL

5

Their
Emotional Wounds

One of the most—if not *the* most—fascinating discoveries I had when I first began working with animals was identifying that they hold the same core emotional wounds as people do, in addition to having the same cloaks of protection.

Defining the
Cloak of Protection

Depending on your animal's past experiences and the physical and emotional wounds birthed from these experiences, your animal may have an unhealed emotional wound that created a feeling of abandonment, betrayal, terror (feeling unsafe), invasiveness, or being detached from his or her core authentic self.

These core wounds can develop from birth trauma, lack of nurturing from one's birth mother, not getting one's needs met, physical trauma, or abuse. Even something that happened that might otherwise be perceived as a minor event can deeply affect how your animal develops and how he or she experiences life. The emotional wounds are held safely under a cloak of protection until the animal feels safe enough to release the perceived pain and negative feelings created by the initial wounding experience. Because emotions are held in the energy field, I see these cloaks as energetic patterns.

At the time the original wound was created, the emotional pain was intentionally pushed down and covered up to safeguard against feeling the emotions birthed from the experience and, in a way, to pretend that it never happened. However, every emotion, positive *and* negative, is filled with life energy, so it will always be reaching for the light so it can be free.

> *Every emotion, positive and negative, is filled*
> *with life energy, so it will always be reaching*
> *for the light so it can be free.*

Covering up emotional wounds is a defense mechanism that could be viewed as ingenious because the animal has yet to develop the internal means to understand and deal with the emotions of the negative experience, so its natural instincts are to disassociate and bury them in the subconscious. However, if the animal is unable to release the cloak as it matures, the emotions from the negative experience will undoubtedly show up as unfounded or exaggerated fears, aggression, detachment, dependence, negative, and/or neurotic behaviors, or even physical issues.

The cloak was beautiful at its inception, given its protective function, but over time it begins to get dingy and gray because it's also concealing the most authentic self and preventing the animal from experiencing a more peaceful and loving life.

From a bioenergetics standpoint, the cloaks of protection unfortunately create energy pathways that your animal's psyche travels time and time again, repeating the same painful pattern, which then triggers the same chemical responses of fear and anxiety. These responses then become habitual and a feeling of normalcy and comfort can even ensue when the same situation continues to present itself. All of this is choreographed and designed to protect the animal from feeling the pain of the original wound.

Think about the rescue animal that has been rehomed and returned time and again to the shelter, or an animal that is triggered into aggressive behavior in repetitive, similar situations. When the animal is able to heal and release the negative feelings stemming from the original wound, it then feels safe enough to allow its authentic self to shine through.

Your Core Emotional Wounds Are Mirrored

Predictable characteristics and potential behaviors are connected with each specific unhealed emotional wound in your animal, making it easier to identify the core wound that they're protecting.

Here's the big insight about your relationship with your animal: You will call into your life and be attracted to an animal that has the same emotional core wound(s) as you do. It's impossible for this not to happen. You will be drawn to each other like magnets. And although the way in which hidden wounds show up for both of you might differ, there will be undeniable similarities. If you didn't get your needs met when you were young, you'll end up with an animal that didn't either. If you've experienced invasiveness, someone doing something to you against your will, your animal will mirror that as well.

The good news is that animals are not as attached to their emotional scars as people are. I've found that they can clear the effects of the original wound much quicker than people. They are more trusting of the energetic healing process as a natural one and are not as attached to holding on to their cloaks of protection because they live more from the right side of their brain than people do.

Details of each emotional wound and the repercussions of the specific cloak that protects it will be explained in further detail to help you gain the knowledge that will allow you to enhance your animal's quality of life in the short run and in the long run. Understanding the animal profiles and their wounds will give you an opportunity to have more love, compassion, and patience for yourself and your animal companion as you continue to evolve together.

Just as people usually have more than one unhealed core emotional wound, animals typically do too. Thus they create experiences at a soul level to help them to simultaneously heal several wounds. When you read through the five descriptive animal profile types that I developed, know that your animal will rarely exhibit 100 percent of the behaviors from any one cloak of protection profile. Out of the five, they'll typically have one or two of the core wounds that are deeper wounds.

Essential Wisdom

The ability to recognize your animals' core emotional wounds could be the beginning of an amazing healing journey for you both to profoundly improve your lives. You've attracted each other so that you can heal together and create a safe environment of love and well-being.

The Scared One

The core wound of the Scared One is rooted in terror, creating a belief in the animal that it's not safe to be here. Typically, these animals have a heightened state of fear and/or exhibit aggression due to a trauma that occurred early in their lives. These young souls are the tremblers in the corner that think people (and/or maybe even other animals) are not safe. Their responses of fear/aggression to a situation can appear to be exaggerated for they are unable to interpret experiences accurately when their emotional wounds have been triggered.

The Scared Ones are very ungrounded because of the distorted belief, created from the original wound, that the world is not safe. The trauma they experienced can be anything from not having been accepted by their birth mothers, to having been bait animals, to even having been attacked or abused by another animal or a person early in their life. This heightened level of fearful behavior might have been modeled and passed down energetically from the Scared One's birth mother if she was in terror at any time during her pregnancy or when nursing her newborn.

The Scared Ones will frequently have thin, weak-looking bodies and eyes that are glazed over, as if they aren't really here; they will usually avoid direct eye contact. They can also have paw/hoof and leg issues since their energy fields are typically raised and as such, are less capable of protecting their lower extremities.

When these animals are not protecting themselves or shaking under the bed if there are visitors or other animals in the house, they usually have very busy, anxious-type behaviors in general. They will frequently be loners when it comes to interactions with other animals in a house environment or rescue center, but if with a pack or herd, they will usually be the obedient followers and low man on the totem pole.

The natural reaction to these animals from animal loving people with good intentions is that they want to reach out and smother them with love so that they will feel safe and begin to have an easier go of things. My experience has been that these animals tend to respond very well to distance energy healing from their own home or stable where they are more comfortable than they are in an unfamiliar setting or with strangers in their presence. Physical interactions are more difficult for them.

Specifically, I've found that facilitating animal sessions with them over the phone enhances their productivity, as this allows them to relax in their safe and familiar environment so they can surrender into the healing process. Then the animals will begin to allow in grounding energy at the pace of their choosing. This helps them to feel more peaceful and safe. Sometimes the core emotional wound can be healed very quickly with The Scared Ones.

The key to working with animals that have experienced a major terror trauma is to be slow and steady in all of your contact with them. They will be teaching you patience in every way possible. You must respect their need for a safe place and a safe pace and resist trying to pull them out of the closet to "face their fears." This will not help their healing process, instead it may well hinder it.

I've seen many animals with this emotional wound end up at rescue centers where oftentimes there is not a safe space for them to heal properly, especially if they are living in a shelter run, crate, or other contained space with visuals to people and other animals. More often than not, these are the animals that are deemed unadoptable simply because there is neither time nor ideal space to allow their healing transformation to take place.

On one level these animals are typically very intelligent but their fear and aggression can be challenging. With the proper patience, including a kind, loving, and quiet atmosphere, they can heal much quicker than people anticipate. That said, the depth of the emotional wound caused by the trauma determines how quickly they will heal. They have to begin to feel safe enough to allow the feeling of being grounded to be their new normal. Again, this can definitely happen with the right environment and approach.

Eddie, the Bedlington Terrier

Marj contacted me about her new animal companion, Eddie, whom she'd recently adopted. Eddie had been sorely abused by a man that had purchased and returned him to a breeder. The breeder said she couldn't sell Eddie because he was so fearful, so the terrier was given away for free to Marj.

Marj stated that Eddie was always fearful and quickly ran to hide when there were any guests in the house. She also sensed that he was somewhat depressed and angry. His interactions with people were consistently marked by fear. He also did not do well with children. Eddie didn't even enjoy his beautiful fenced-in backyard. Every sound and neighbor's dog sent him running inside, terrified, to get back to his safe place.

After Eddie's first session, Marj noticed immediate and positive changes in his behavior. Even Marj's friends mentioned that he seemed more relaxed and friendly. To do her part, Marj consistently gave him more space, did not force Eddie to come out of hiding when visitors were present, and reinforced any positive, courageous steps she saw him taking, however small they were. She provided a very patient and loving atmosphere in which he could feel safe to love again. After our third session, Eddie lay calmly outside while other animals walked by him and barked. In fact, he even stood and defended his property if that's what was called for. Marj described him as acting empowered; finally at peace.

Eddie is a great example of how the right environment can quickly heal an animal and release a past trauma so that the animal can get grounded in their authentic self and have an easier life experience.

Marj also learned a lot about herself in the process of having to be extra patient with Eddie. She realized that he was mirroring a part of herself that was fearful of letting people get close to her. It also came into her awareness that she had a very strong inner critic and beat herself up a lot. She said that going through the process with Eddie helped her to be kinder to herself and to feel more empowered too.

How to Help the Scared Ones Heal

1. These animals need physical movement (*if* they enjoy it—don't force them), as it will help them to release their excess fearful energy. Walking in nature is the best type of physical activity for them, because Mother Earth can help to ground them. Playing with them is also a great option that induces physical movement and helps them begin to feel safe in your company.

2. They need a safe place to retreat to when they feel scared. Respect their space and the timing needed to trust you. When they exhibit even the slightest improvement, praise them; tell them how brave they are and that you are proud of their courage to change. Small steps are a big deal for these animals.

3. Show them patience and resist forcing them into social situations. Accepting them where they are is key for them to heal and for them to begin to believe that they can feel safe and begin to have a better quality of life.
4. Make sure your thoughts are focused on the positive. Instead of replaying the story (to yourself and others) of how scared they are, see them as adjusting and getting braver every day. Focus on any positive shifts in their behavior and visualize them being surrounded with love.
5. Resist the urge to overlove them, which will feel invasive and could cause them to retreat further. Ultimately they need to feel independent and secure in their own bodies to allow the grounding they need to feel safe enough to trust again.

The Sensitive One

These animals are also known by yours truly as the Sponges because they will absorb the energy and emotions from their people (and others). These sensitive animals have an emotional wound that was created from invasiveness or from being overcontrolled very early on in their lives.

Like the Scared Ones, they may frequently hide because they aren't comfortable being in social situations, but it's for a different reason. It's because these overly sensitive animals are feeling *everyone's* energy because they have very weak boundaries. They might want to observe from afar but will be keenly aware of each guest's energy, sensing and knowing who they really are at their core.

Yet with their beloved person, whom they trust, they want to and will be all over you—especially when you're upset. This is because they want to help you heal. And they're phenomenal healers because they're very intuitive, sensitive, and have the ability to accurately read others. However, until their own emotional wound is healed, they can be almost clingy because they haven't fully developed their individuated self.

The Sensitive Ones' human companions will unconsciously tend to be more invasive with them—for example, picking them up when they don't want to be held and/or carrying them around against their will. These animals are people pleasers, so you might not even know they are building up resentment and then pushing it down. Animals with overcontrolled backgrounds have relatively passive personalities so their guardians will actually think they know what their sensitive animals want. However, this is not always true.

These animals are also frequently overeaters because subconsciously they are trying to compensate for their lack of boundaries. In some of them, more so in dogs, one might see their repressed negative energy come out during feeding time with the other animals—they don't believe there will be enough food for them.

Because they don't typically retaliate to any invasiveness perpetrated upon them, they suppress emotions, which might show up by them piddling in inappropriate places. This is a sign they are suppressing anger, which could create cystitis or problems in the bladder or kidneys. Please realize that this is just their repressed emotions, and/or emotions they absorbed from their people, which need to be cleared. They might also have dental or gum issues created by the suppression of their authentic feelings. Since they are sponges for your energy, they could mirror your physical issues as well.

When you take them to the vet, they will hide in your

armpit but will let the technicians and veterinarian do what they need to do without fighting because they don't believe they have a choice. They will feel empowered to make choices when they begin healing their core wound.

Situations that could have caused the wound of invasiveness might have been at the hands of a breeder or even a rescue center that kept them in a small environment and didn't let them develop their own sense of self, which typically occurs when they experience more freedom. There could also have been a person who overcontrolled them in a negative way or smothered them with fear-based love. If you've ever watched a mother with her offspring, she will not smother the newborns but models good boundaries and protects them when needed, while still allowing them to find their own way to independence and to getting their own needs met.

The Sensitive Ones don't think they have any rights and don't know how to adequately express themselves, nor do they have good boundaries. In other words, they don't believe they can be who they really are because they were never really allowed to develop their sense of self in a formative phase, which for cats and dogs, is typically a period of two to five months.

Matisse, the American Shorthair Cat

When Tonya went to pick out her new kitten, she fell in love at first sight and named him Matisse. She'd lost two pets in the months before and needed this kitten to shower her love on. He was her baby, and she hung tightly onto him, smothering him with love and developing a codependent relationship with him.

By the time Matisse was a young adult he had gum issues (requiring dental cleanings twice yearly) and chronic urinary tract infections, which materialized several times with stones and crystals. Matisse would also hide under the bed when there were visitors in the house. Tonya described him as her "sensitive love muffin" and expressed a heightened state of fear about any suffering he might undergo. She was also terrified that he might die early as her two previous pets had done, which she believed would be devastating.

Tonya wanted to schedule an energetic healing session for Matisse as soon as possible because he had confirmed stones in his bladder, a urinary tract infection, and a temperature of 104 degrees. Apparently he'd had a negative reaction to mainstream medication, so she'd taken him off it and was instead working frantically to provide relief to him and to help him heal.

Upon connecting with Matisse for his first session, it was difficult to tell where his energy stopped and Tonya's began. They were enmeshed energetically, and my sense was that there was strong mirroring in place that pertained to their core emotional wounds.

During treatment, Matisse released a lot of suppressed resentment held in his bladder, and I could also feel codependent energetic cords between the two of them being released. He responded very well to the energy work; I could feel his bladder healing physically as well. Matisse received three sessions in one week, and during the second session I saw the stones in his bladder being broken up and cleared.

Tonya saw a dramatically positive shift in Matisse, which made his mama very happy. She had scheduled a prearranged follow-up appointment with the vet and was tempted to cancel it, however, she realized that she was curious to see what she would say. Much to the vet's surprise, the stones *were gone, and Matisse's temperature was back to normal.*

I discussed with Tonya the importance of allowing Matisse the space to reveal his authentic self and to give him the space and patience to heal his emotional wounds. I also decided to carefully ask her if she had any invasiveness in her background or if she had been overcontrolled. Indeed she was. As a result, Tonya began receiving energy sessions almost weekly for quite some time.

We spoke many years later, and I asked about Matisse. Tonya shared that he was doing great and never again had had a urinary tract infection or dental or gum issues. She seemed much more grounded and confident in herself and was very committed to her personal and spiritual growth, which I know greatly contributed to Matisse feeling better as well.

How to Help the Sensitive Ones Heal

1. Respect and honor their wishes instead of exhibiting a tendency to be invasive with them, even with minor issues such as choosing a toy, going outside, or determining where they should lie down. Be patient while they are beginning to make decisions on their own and eventually, the amount of time it takes for them to make a decision will shorten.

2. Give them space. If they prefer not to socialize with houseguests, give them the space to decide if and when they want to socialize with new people. If you honor them in this way and release the need for them to *be* a certain way, they'll increasingly begin to come out of hiding more frequently on their own. Praise them when they do.

3. Help them to get grounded. They typically long for

sunshine and you may find them lounging around outside or in that spot of sun beaming in through the window, as it helps them feel more grounded and connected. They are very sensitive, and this time in nature and being in the sun is much like a healing session for them.

4. Apologize to them. You might have unconsciously fallen into an invasive habit by being overcontrolling or smothering them. However, you're human, and this new level of your awareness is just coming in. If you apologize to them, it can shift the energy of the relationship to a healthier one. Also say to them, "You are free to be you. I will honor who you are. I honor the magnificent and authentic being of light that is you."

5. Make time for your own conscious healing around the issues of overcontrol, smothering, and humiliation, for your animals will benefit immensely. This is especially true of the Sensitive Ones. Because of their weaker boundaries, the energy of these animals tends to be enmeshed with that of their people, and they both need to heal so they can feel safe enough to reveal their authentic selves.

The Protector

It'll be easy to identify which animal is using the protector profile, because they'll be highly visible—in your face at the fence or the first one to greet you at the door. At their core, the wound they are protecting originated in a betrayal, usually by someone they knew and cared about.

These animals believe they need to be proactive to ensure they are never betrayed again. At every turn they'll try to tell you that another animal or person is someone you should be leery of. They might even attack them in a misguided attempt to ensure their own safety and survival. Their third eye, or intuitive center, got out of balance when they were betrayed early on, so they do not accurately interpret who is potentially dangerous and who is not. They would never consciously see themselves as bullies, because in the midst of their aggressive reaction to a situation they believe there is potential for a life-or-death betrayal to occur. Thus they will overreact, probably with aggression, given that they're motivated to armor up, protect, and serve.

It won't be difficult to hear them either, for they will intentionally be vocal in an attempt to be intimidating. They naturally feel it's their job to protect the house, the yard, their guardian and—mostly—themselves. These animals have a difficult time trusting, as they are so used to being on the defensive and assuming that danger is imminent. They work hard to control their environment as best they can.

One of the first clues that your animals are using this particular cloak of protection is indicated by your inclination to either tell them they're bad or believe that they're bad. If you have many animals, you'll assume *the Protector* was responsible when you find the garbage can knocked over, and in turn, was "bad." This is because their unhealed emotional patterns will unconsciously cause you to make them the scapegoat. And most of the time, they *are* the perpetrator of the action.

Their negative behaviors are actually derived from their distorted beliefs that they really are bad. This will set in motion a continual (unconscious) cycle of them trying to continue to prove this to you. Your confirming to them that their behavior is indeed bad only serves to perpetuate the negative behavior. You will have to consciously break the cycle so they can see their light.

All souls have a magnificent spark of the Divine in them, and these beautiful animals are no exception. If they trust you, you have already seen that light. They can be very sweet and gentle. Mostly they're fiercely loyal companions—almost to a fault. They have pushed down their emotional pain and with it their vulnerability. They secretly long to heal and release the pain.

Energetically, they are ungrounded. They hold most of their energy at their shoulders and head because they want to be prepared to attack at a moment's notice. Given this, they are prone to hip problems or issues with their back legs.

These animals can heal with the right loving environment, but sometimes their human companions consciously or unconsciously like the overprotection they are receiving from the Protector. There is a part of them that is proud and boasts about their nonwimpy animal. Yet this is where the mirroring comes in, for what you see in them is also in you. You might see the world as a scary place and welcome the protection due to your own unhealed wounds of betrayal. That can delay your ability to provide them with an optimum healing environment.

If you have an animal that overprotects you and maybe even frightens other people away from getting close to you, I highly suggest that you explore energy healing sessions for you both. Your overprotecting animal could be telling you that you have repressed anger and a betrayal wound that needs to be healed and released.

Remember, embedded in your animal's actions and behaviors there is always a gift trying to reveal itself. Many times animals with betrayal wounds are mirroring for their people something they do not want to look at or, in other words, a part of yourself that you judge. Once you raise your awareness and see the gifts that your animal brings you for your personal healing, his or her behavior will settle down and become much more peaceful.

Buster, the Labrador Retriever Mix

During the period of time that I was leading the animal ministry at my spiritual community, I received a call from a young family. Apparently they were moving out of state the following week and couldn't take their dog Buster with them. They were hopeful the animal ministry team could help Buster find a new, wonderful home. Victoria, his two-legged mom, was beside herself in having to make the decision to rehome Buster. She'd tried everything she could think of and felt her options were running out.

She and her husband were expecting their second child, and they already had a two-year-old. The main reason for their decision to not take Buster with them was because he had bitten their toddler twice in the few months prior. Victoria and her husband dearly loved Buster, but they feared he'd bite their child again. They tried many things to help their beloved dog overcome his negative behavior, but decided they just couldn't risk keeping him, especially with the second baby coming.

When they initially adopted Buster, they were able to give him a lot of attention. However, he'd always been the protector of the house and had also shown aggression with other dogs on their walks. I could feel Victoria's fear. I also got the sense Buster might be behind bringing about the changes (that the move would entail) for the highest good of all. At a soul level, there is always a bigger plan at work trying to get the right and perfect people and animals together for the betterment of all.

As it happened (there are never any coincidences), the very next day I shared Buster's photo and story with my colleague, Ruby. After discussing the matter with her husband, Ruby said they were very interested in meeting Buster. The meet and greet went very well and, at the very least, they agreed to foster Buster so he wouldn't have to be turned in to the animal shelter.

Ruby's only concern was that they had an elder indoor cat whom they dearly loved, and they worried that Buster would negatively affect her. Ruby and her husband had very grounding energy and worked patiently to train Buster so that his triggers and reactions from the past would be transmuted.

They quickly fell in love with him and decided to keep him permanently. Indeed, he did chase their cat, Trinity, so Ruby and her husband kept them in separate areas of their home when gone. While going through this period of helping Buster heal his emotional wounds, they consistently employed compassionate training methods, which he responded to very well.

After showing him consistent patience, compassion, and love, he softened, healed, and began to trust again. Buster also received six energy healing clearings during those first few months to help him release his early emotional pain.

After several months, Buster and Trinity were able to be left alone together. Sometimes they would even lie on the sofa next to each other, which was quite the achievement and reflected just how much Buster had healed his past emotional wounds. When Ruby and her husband had a baby, they had no fears about Buster's behavior. Buster lived out the rest of his years peacefully, having felt the love of two

families. Victoria stayed in touch with Ruby and her hus-
band, and when Buster passed on, both families mourned
him and honored his transition.

How to Help the Protectors Heal

1. These animals really need your patience, as it takes time for them to let down their guard so that that their deeply held pain can be released. Then they can heal their emotional wound of feeling betrayed and begin to believe and know that they are good at their core.

2. It can be difficult to *not* call these animals bad, as they can appear to be trying hard to convince you of exactly that. Giving them unconditional love and acceptance will help tremendously. Avoid making them the scapegoat. (In fact, take the b-word out of your descriptions of all of your animals.)

3. Release your anger in healthy ways instead of directing it at them, for that will not resolve the situation. If you do direct your anger at them, they will most likely absorb it and mirror it back to you.

4. Giving more attention to their positive behaviors instead of their undesired actions is probably the most powerful tool at your disposal to help them change. Then they can more easily begin to break down the barriers of this potentially exhausting cloak of protection. They will then be more mature and less easily triggered. Tell them they are lovable. Tell them they are good. Tell them you see their light within.

5. Believe in them. Have faith in their ability to heal and change, and they will begin to trust and let their kindest selves be increasingly revealed, to people and other animals alike. If you meditate (or even if you don't), visualize

your animal during your meditation time, and see them feeling grounded and at peace.

6. Find compassion for them. This will help to release the more vulnerable, loyal, and kind aspects of them. They wouldn't be how they are without having suffered in the past. Both of you will feel better if you find it within yourself to be compassionate.

The Needy One

This most frequently used cloak of protection is concealing the unhealed wound of abandonment. As you can imagine, animals are all too frequently abandoned and this can affect them all differently. Some of these animals may have been emotionally or physically abandoned many times. The cycle may well continue until they begin to heal from the fact that they did not receive vitally important nurturing from their birth mother.

More specifically, the feeling of abandonment began when they did not get to nurse from their birth mother to the point of feeling full. This can happen in many different ways. It could be that something happened to the mother to prevent this. Or the mother refused to let the newborn nurse, or maybe the wee one was edged out by its siblings.

The newborn needs to attain the feeling of being full when nursing—to the point that it chooses to detach from its mother on its own. There is an energy flow between the newborn and its mother that is much like a spiritual high. During this time they are connected until the newborn feels full. In that moment they are actually feeling not only each other's divinity, but also the spiritual flow of love from God. It's such an important time and connection to have experienced because it imparts the knowledge, psychologically and emotionally, that there will always *be* enough (food, love, and attention), that they *are* enough, *and* that they are lovable.

Animals that were blessed to have received the sensation of being full will simply stop eating at that point and will not overeat. Many, many animals and people never know this feeling, however, and as a result, they struggle throughout their lives to get their needs met. *The outer world is always a reflection of the beliefs of the inner world.*

I frequently call this profile the *not-enough syndrome* with my clients. It shows up in their animals' behaviors in ways that are easy to identify. Think of the dog that chases the tennis ball until he can hardly walk or the cat that will eat as if it will never have food again. They are always seeking to be filled externally because they never acquired the sensation of knowing when they feel full.

The same insatiable need to be filled is also happening at an energetic level. They are feeding on your energy in an endless battle to feel full because they don't know how to fill themselves energetically and retain the energy. They must learn to self-fill from within by feeling firmly grounded into Mother Earth and connected to the heart and mind of God in order to begin to know that they really are lovable. People sometimes don't mind giving them the extra affection, but many people are annoyed by their unquenchable needs. The Needy Ones' continual feeling of being starved for something to fill them can also contribute to the creation of having a codependent relationship with their human companions.

Separation anxiety is also a result of these animals not having the healthy oral developmental stage that comes with nursing. If the animal doesn't heal the emotional wound of abandonment and learn how to fill itself with the love it seeks externally, it will show up as an oral fixation. Any obsessive behavior involving the mouth derives from the animal having felt abandoned in its past. Some of these behaviors are obsessive licking, overchewing, excessive "talking" (barking/meowing, etc), sucking on items or even people, overeating, carrying around a toy (or other item) all the time, and/or frequent nipping or cribbing (horses).* These animals will always look you in the eye and try to connect deeply with you so that they can get energy from you in a way they did not from their birth mother.

They are typically social and will be happy to greet your guests to grab attention and energy from them too. They can also be jealous when you give affection to another and try to manipulate your time. Until their emotional wound is healed, these animals are likely to be repeatedly abandoned. Their energy will set up the continuous cycle, with each rehoming or loss of a loved one reinforcing a distorted unconscious belief that they are indeed unlovable.

They are usually ungrounded and, overall, have small energy fields since they're unable to retain energy. Physically, they can be susceptible to jaw or dental issues, gastrointestinal problems—especially stomach, gallbladder, and pancreas—and they could have weight issues.

In a healthy environment where they can learn that they're lovable, they will gradually heal as they get used to holding more energy and begin to learn how to fill themselves. Then they will be able to release the deeper emotional pain of grief and loss created from their abandonment. Their healing will

---

*A horse who cribs uses its teeth to grab on to a solid object and repetitively suck in air. This habitual movement releases endorphins which make the horse want to repeat the activity.

be much faster if you as their human companion can be proactive in healing *your* abandonment wounds so that you will know how to fill yourself and in turn promote a healthier, more independent relationship between you and your pet.

Jetson, the English Bulldog Mix

Jetson had been rehomed more than once, and like most rescued dogs, his history was unknown. Mary Ann shared that Jetson had a tendency to latch on to a person's garments for dear life when people visited him in his run at the no-kill shelter. He wouldn't let go, as if pleading with his visitors to adopt him. Ultimately his neediness appeared aggressive, which concerned those who might have been interested in adopting him. The rescue organization felt that a home environment would be more conducive for Jetson, and Mary Ann volunteered to foster him.

Much like when a puppy is first adjusting after leaving its birth mother and siblings, Jetson would also frequently whine and whimper, which is a clear sign that he didn't know what it felt like to be full when nursed by his birth mom. Mary Ann quickly found out that he didn't tolerate being around other dogs well because he wanted 100 percent of her attention, and he ate as if every meal was his last one, always wanting more. He also would be very proactive in defending his food bowl when her other dogs were around. Eventually, keeping Jetson became too difficult for Mary Ann—she continually felt drained around him, and keeping the dogs apart was very challenging in her home. Thus she sought out another organization that would take him in.

Jetson ended up being moved to another no-kill center, and a woman named Erin was his new foster guardian. Erin quickly learned about Jetson's food-protection issues at mealtime. He also wouldn't let Erin out of his sight and constantly followed her around, wanting to be glued to her. However, Erin found herself drawn to his inner light and saw the loving dog that he was at his core.

He was on the adoptable list at her organization and Erin found herself growing increasingly attached to Jetson because he fulfilled a need for her as well. She had an unconscious need to be needed, and their energy quickly enmeshed as their unhealed wounds drew them together like magnets. Erin wanted to be a savior to Jetson. She felt he'd been misunderstood, and Erin frequently felt misunderstood, too.

When a nice woman put in an application to adopt him, Erin had mixed emotions. Of course she wanted the highest and best for Jetson, but her inner child's heart had gotten attached to the adoring dog, and she was as overprotective of him as he was of his next meal. And she didn't want him to go through being rehomed again if things didn't work out. However, Erin had to admit that having Jetson in her home had indeed been challenging due to the extra time his care took and the need to keep him separated from the other dogs at mealtime.

During Jetson's healing sessions, I could feel him allowing more love into his heart, and I believe this was due to Erin's acceptance of and patience with him. Much grief and loss that had derived from his early life was released during the sessions. Erin had also gone through much loss, and given this, it was clear that one of the gifts of their relationship was to help each other heal and release grief.

Erin and I discussed the possibility of her taking Jetson to meet the applicant in an in-home visit, based on the fact that her conversations with the woman had gone very well.

She lived alone with no other animals in the house and worked from home. Erin was emotionally torn about possibly giving Jetson up but knew that it would be clear to her if it was meant to be. I suggested that she ask Jetson to give her signs if he wanted to live with the woman.

Once at the new woman's house, Jetson gave Erin both of the exact signs she'd asked him for. She'd told him to roll in the grass, something he hadn't done for a while but had loved doing in the past. And she also asked him to jump up on the sofa and get comfortable; another thing he loved doing. When he jumped up on the sofa and laid his head on his new mom's lap, Erin knew for sure that Jetson wanted to live with this woman.

She couldn't deny, even though her heart was breaking, that he was giving her permission to let him go. She knew she needed to give him up, to put Jetson's need for an attentive home above her own need to be needed. Jetson's new mom and Erin stayed in touch, and he was never returned or abandoned again. He lived out the rest of his life knowing what it felt like to be filled with love. Erin still reflects on the time they had together and how meaningful it was for her healing journey, and Jetson's as well.

How to Help the Needy Ones Heal

1. Make an intention to help them become more independent. Resist giving them constant attention and overloving them. They are typically feeding on energy from your stomach area, known energetically as your solar plexus or power center, which can leave you feeling drained. You can put your hand over your stomach as a reminder to retain your energy while still letting them know they are loved.

2. Visualize them having the sense of feeling full by seeing love flowing through them from both Mother Earth and God. See them beginning to retain more and more of this love each day.

3. They need to know that they are lovable, so assure them that they are sparks of the Divine and are enough just as they are.

4. Make sure they have some alone time even when you're home so they can begin to develop a healthier sense of self and not be dependent on you for their happiness.

5. At a deeper level, they need to release repressed feelings of grief and loss, so if they suffer the loss of a family member or a buddy, let them take the time they need to grieve. (Read more on this in Chapter Eleven, "Easing through Change.")

6. Take at least five minutes a day to fill yourself with love by placing your hands on your heart and imagining divine love from the heavens flowing into it, filling you in a way you have not allowed before. Connect to your angels if this is easier and let them fill you. Begin a conscious process of knowing that *you* are loveable and that *you* are enough just as you are.

The Perfect One

We've made it to the very interesting profile from which many master-healer animals are birthed. Often described as being the good dog (cat, horse, etc.), these old souls are always grounded but lack a solid connection with their true essence and authenticity.

The Perfect Ones were likely to have been born from a mother who was also disconnected from her true essence with her litter/offspring. Some animals of this profile could have been born with this emotional cloak solely to have a higher purpose and intention of helping/serving others. Still others may have been adopted by a person who, early on, began training them to be the perfect companion.

From early in their lives these Perfect Ones were trained where to sit and how to act appropriately in every situation. They learned to be "perfect" to the outside world, while simultaneously denying their real selves. They are driven to be the best they can be and are continually praised for acting appropriately in most situations, as they know no other way to be. By a long shot, the Perfect Ones derive more perks than the other four profiles (because everyone constantly tells the animal that it is good).

Through their training to be a perfect companion, they experienced a detachment from their real selves and became somewhat robotic. They are rarely overly warm and fuzzy with their guardians because they are acting as they were taught to act, and are unable to connect to their person with their whole heart. You are drawn to them because of their calm behaviors and demeanor but when you pet them and try to connect, you may feel a lack of a heart connection with them.

These animals are also the ones that keep order in the house, on the property, or in the barn. They usually aren't happy unless everything is as it should be and will gently correct other animals if they act inappropriately. They will not become codependent with their person or have any negative behaviors. Physical ailments are few and far between, however, if and when an ailment does occur it is likely to present as muscular diseases or spine or heart issues.

Much like a guru will do, some of these animals may intentionally take on the ailments and diseases of people (or other animals) simply to ease the suffering of another soul. Usually they can move out the energy they absorbed from the person because of their great connection to Mother Earth, but as they get older this can be harder for them to do on their own.

These animals have a more tenuous connection with love. It's not that they don't have the ability to love, because they do, but they aren't as deeply connected to their hearts as some of the other animal profiles are. They have protection in place to keep from feeling love more intimately, but this also keeps their divine essence under lock and key, which prevents them from receiving the spiritual high of divine love flowing through them.

Rarely will these animals want to sit on your lap and lick your face, thereby exclaiming that you're God's gift to them. *The more consciously aware guardians of these animals will feel a deep soul connection with them. There will be a knowing between the two of them that they signed up together for a higher purpose.* These higher-vibrating animals and their guardians are both doers by nature, as they both like growing and learning new things.

The Perfect Ones tend to use more of the left side of their brain than animals of the other profile types. They have more thinking skills and are more balanced energetically between thinking and feeling.

Most everyone has seen these animals because they are shown in competitions, have mastered agility training, or they are working animals such as police or military dogs. My personal favorite, these are also the animals that are master healers and therapy animals, on a divine mission to bring light and healing to people, including children, the elderly, and even those in prison.

You have probably seen their people as well. Typically they are grounded, responsible overachievers who have very polished appearances and always have the right words at their disposal. At times they may be overcontrolling and often might have a difficult time understanding why others don't act appropriately. They are usually great leaders, very visible, and take action to achieve their goals and dreams . . . one after the other.

If the guardians of these animals have embraced a more spiritual path that includes a self-healing journey, then both the person and their animal will feel and experience more compassion and vulnerability in their lives. The Perfect Ones make up the smallest percentage of my animal client base because they don't exhibit many negative behaviors or have many physical ailments until they become seniors. When helping them heal through energy sessions, it often takes some time for them to begin releasing some of the armor around their hearts to reveal more and more of their authentic selves. The goal is to hold space to allow them to get back in touch with their divine essences so they can have more authentic experiences.

Even after these animals have transitioned, I will sometimes continue to feel them around me when I am facilitating a session and get the sense they are assisting me from the other side.

Read below for several incredible stories of animals that I have been blessed to know who employ this particular cloak of protection.

Sage, the Feral Tabby Kitten

I will never forget one particular litter of very feral kittens. I was able to catch the first four of the five siblings easily and brought them into my home for their domestication and to help them find loving families. I have always loved observing the different personalities of newborns in litters and their interactions. One of the kittens, Sage, was always very grounded and was much less fearful than the others. He was the calm one and the wise one that the other kittens clearly respected.

The other kittens all wanted to be around him, and they emulated his actions. Sage was always the first kitten to play with the toy, test out the new bed, and allow human touch. The others watched and learned from his actions. I could tell he knew, at some level, the importance of his role, but he maintained a healthy level of detachment from his littermates.

When I was finally able to catch the fifth kitten, Braveheart, and bring him inside to join the other four, I worried how the rest of the litter would react to him. It had been a couple of weeks since they'd seen each other. With all of the different smells, would they hiss at Braveheart and not accept him? I put him in a crate, which I brought into the kittens' room in the house. Then I quietly opened its doors, stood back, and observed the interactions between the kittens and their long-lost brother.

While all of the other kittens were hiding, Sage immediately recognized his brother trembling in fear and walked into the crate and casually greeted him. It looked as if he was calmly filling Braveheart in about their new situation and assuring him that everything would be okay. Then Sage turned and approached each of the other siblings. He seemed to be coaxing them to also welcome their very scared brother, to ease his transition to the new environment. This was fascinating to watch. One by one, Sage walked with each sibling into the crate to reintroduce them to Braveheart. There were times during this amazing experience that I held my breath and tears flowed down my cheeks, for I felt as though I was witnessing something sacred. Braveheart then felt comforted and safe enough to move out of the crate and join his siblings.

It was no surprise that Sage was the first kitten to be adopted by a young couple. I knew he would be fine with whomever he was with, but I worried that the couple was of a young partying age, and Sage was not used to that type of atmosphere. Their application and references were wonderful, though, so I decided to let him go home with them the following weekend.

His new guardians, Jason and Emily, kept in touch for the remainder of the first year for they knew that Sage was near and dear to my heart. Every picture they sent me of him brought a smile to my face, for I could see how happy they all were together. Indeed, it was a match made in heaven. In one photo, Sage was wrapped around Jason's shoulders like a scarf. He looked blissfully comfortable and content. He was still the grounded, wise one.

They changed his name to Chief, which was also very appropriate. Emily shared that whenever there were a lot of guests in their apartment, Chief was comfortably in the center of the action. Their friends all said the same thing: "I have never liked cats before, but now I do after meeting Chief."

The experience made me realize the importance of his adoption into an environment where he could reach and touch many hearts. He's a teacher and was driven by a higher purpose from the moment he was born. I am blessed and better for having known him.

Alex, the Labrador Retriever

Alex is one of the greeter Ambassadogs at Unity North Atlanta Spiritual Community in Marietta, Georgia. Sue, her guardian, leads their animal ministry. I got to know Alex during the monthly Praying Paws Animal Service, when Sue asked me to facilitate the monthly message and meditation. I couldn't help but notice how much Alex's personality and actions fit the profile of the Perfect One. Alex is always very calm and lets everyone approach and love her. Yet her personality is somewhat detached, which is typical of master healers.

Alex was initially adopted as a puppy by a man who had put her through a lot of training. When the gentleman began traveling for his job, he tied Alex to a doghouse in his backyard to fend for herself when he was out of town. Neighbors would make sure she had basic needs like food and water.

The man's sister intervened to find Alex a new home, and she called Sue to see if she would consider adding another dog to their family. Sue and her husband, Bill, had two older dogs, and were concerned about keeping the peace in a household with three dogs. Ultimately, they decided to give it a try, and of course Alex, being very grounded, was easily accepted by the other two dogs and fit in perfectly.

Given Sue's strong desire to serve and help others, Alex has truly flourished and embraced her life purpose of helping other souls heal and feel loved. Alex has been with Sue for seven years and has quite the résumé. She is a certified therapy dog with Happy Tails Pet Therapy, an organization that connects volunteers and their animals with people who enjoy physical, social, emotional, and cognitive benefits from their visit. In addition to visiting two nursing homes each week, Alex also visits the children's rehab center at Scottish Rite Hospital in Atlanta, where the children can pet her or throw a toy, which helps in their recovery. They also visit Peachford Hospital, a psychiatric children's hospital in Atlanta, where the children share their thoughts and feelings with Alex. Most recently, they've added Reading Paws to their list. This is a national organization wherein animals go to libraries and schools to help children develop confidence while reading books to the dogs.

My heart overflows with gratitude to contemplate the myriad of people Alex has touched with Sue's help. They are a very powerful healing duo, and they were clearly meant to be together.

Lily, the Westie-Cairn Terrier Mix

Anyaa McAndrew is a therapist in North Carolina who specializes in helping women heal and embrace their divine feminine, authentically beautiful selves. She facilitates women's groups throughout the United States and also internationally. Her dog Lily traveled with her and joined her when she facilitated the weekend intensive groups; she and Anyaa were a healing team.

Lily had a fan club of those who had been touched and healed by her presence in the healing circles that Anyaa facilitated. The stories were amazing! During the intensives, as the stories were being shared, Lily would sit in the center of the circle of women and instinctively walk over to the woman who most needed her gifts of healing, and she would literally absorb her pain.

I began working with Lily in the last few years of her life. When I met her, I noticed she was calm and grounded. She was not a dog who would jump up on you or give you continuous slurps in the face. She was kind and dutiful and was, overall, a great companion for Anyaa.

When Anyaa initially contacted me, Lily was in the middle of having an acute pancreatic attack. The veterinarian didn't offer much promise of a recovery from this long-term illness, especially knowing that she was a senior dog.

Lily had other plans, though, as her healing work wasn't yet completed. Lily responded extremely well to the energy healing sessions I facilitated on her. Her level of awareness was very high, and she took full advantage of our time together to embark on a deeper healing journey.

For three more years, until she was fifteen years young, Lily continued her journey to bring more light into the world. However, she got to a point that she needed assistance in releasing all that she had absorbed during the healing circles. Anyaa made sure we always had a session on the calendar the day after the weekend groups.

In each healing session I conducted on Lily, I observed different energetic areas of congestion and physical sensations in her energy that I had never felt during her previous sessions. For example, during a session I might see thyroid issues or self-hate issues releasing out of Lily's energy field. When I shared the information with Anyaa after the session, she would know immediately which woman in the group had arrived with those same issues, and had in turn left feeling healed.

It was hard for Anyaa to see her beloved companion having a slow recovery period after the healing weekends, and she desperately wanted Lily to stop taking on everyone's pain. However, much to Anyaa's dismay, Lily would not discontinue her work. It was part of her spiritual DNA to be a master healer.

Working with Lily those three years was a gift to me and even while she was still on this Earth, I would occasionally feel her presence when doing sessions on other animals. I always had the sense that she was guiding me and assisting in the healing sessions. I will forever be grateful for her teachings in my life.

How to Help the Perfect Ones Heal

1. With the power of your mind, make an intention to connect to your animal companion heart-to-heart and soul-to-soul while sitting with them for a few minutes each day. This will help both of you begin to feel the spark of the Divine within more easily. This will also help to release some of the protection around both of your hearts.

2. Allow your companion to be imperfect, which means to resist overcontrolling them (especially when they're not working).

3. If they are working healers, make sure they get plenty of exercise to move out any energy they have absorbed. As they age, they may need additional help with this.

4. These animals will greatly benefit from massage to help them move the energy out of their muscles so they can relax and release their rigidity.

Essential Wisdom

Your animal will have some of each of the cloak of protection profiles discussed in this chapter, however, there are one to two profiles that they'll more frequently exhibit. Knowing about *their* core emotional wounds can give you additional clues to what *you* are working on healing. Remember, they are your mirror, and you can both heal faster when you raise your awareness to look at the situation from the perspective of your higher self.

All of the advice given herein is designed to help you and your animals heal your emotional wounds from the inside out. Every animal and situation is different, so trust your sense as to what may be the right and perfect path to healing for them and for you. Know that you've attracted each other so that you can heal together. More specifically, I believe that you have a sacred soul contract with each other and in this, you were destined to be together.

The most powerful source of healing for you and your animals is the presence of unconditional love; it is the very foundation of your relationship. Never forget this.

Lily 1994–2009 (with Anyaa)

Nothing ever goes away until it has taught us what we need to know.

PEMA CHODRON

PART FOUR
THE KNOWING

The vital function that pets fulfill in this world hasn't been fully recognized. They keep millions of people sane.

ECKHART TOLLE

6

The Love Bind

It feels like yesterday that I gazed into the beautiful blue eyes of my first pet, the cutest little calico kitten *ever*, and realized she saw no flaws in me—she simply *loved* me. Even though I had a busy work life and many friends, I hadn't *really* let anyone get close to me, and this precious kitten profoundly rocked my world by getting through to my heart when no other soul had been able to break through the protection.

Heck, I didn't even realize my heart was under lock and key until she showed up. Life is like that—something happens, and a new level of awareness presents itself to help you grow and mature. You don't know what you don't know until you know it.

The Power of Unconditional Love

That was the first time I felt the vulnerability that unconditional love can invoke. It arrived with an unexpected secondary gift. It also came into my awareness that up until that point of my life, I believed my relationships always came with strings attached. Be it love, loyalty, acceptance, devotion, material things, or even physical labor—I was suddenly very conscious that I had always felt, at some level, that people expected something in return for their love. And here was this little ray-of-light kitten just simply loving me—the real me—without an agenda. It was refreshing and beautiful and scary. *Yes*, scary.

When my kitten Khalua was three months old, she walked in my bedroom soaking wet and shivering. She had just discovered, and then fallen into, the toilet. Whereas others might have thought the situation a bit humorous, I frantically grabbed a towel to dry her off and then proceeded to kitten-proof the entire apartment. Feeling unconditional love for the first time immediately instilled an innate fear of losing that love, throughout every fiber of my being.

And that's how it begins. Your heart learns about the safety of unconditional love from your animal companions, so you dive in, and get addicted to the feeling the pets bring up within you. In turn, you believe if the pets leave they will take with them the love, acceptance, and joy you feel in your heart. This is especially true if your animals were the only unconditional love you've ever experienced. This can elevate the fear of losing them, especially their love and the feelings of bliss and safety when with them.

Animals are serving an extraordinary role in helping people expand their ability to feel the higher vibrational emotions such as love, joy, compassion, and forgiveness. Sometimes I reflect on where mankind would be without the influence of animals—not only from a physical, evolutionary point of view, but from the standpoint of our emotional growth as well.

> *Animals are serving an extraordinary role*
> *in helping people expand their ability to*
> *feel the higher vibrational emotions.*

People who did not receive proper love and nurturing in their childhood, which is actually most people, may unconsciously tend to cling to love derived from their animal companions more tightly. Or, never fully grieving and healing from an earlier loss can also give birth to a fear-based love relationship with your current pets, because you'll fiercely want to protect your heart from more grief being piled on top of the unhealed wound.

In this chapter, I will more fully explain the energetic causes and effects of hidden underlying fears that may be embedded in the deep love you have for your animals. Sometimes just raising your awareness is all that's needed for positive shifts to unfold in the relationship.

The Inner Dynamics of Overloving

Do any of the following seem familiar to you?

- Overcontrolling your animal companions.
- Overprotecting them.
- Overfeeding them.
- Overnurturing or coddling them.
- Overloving them.
- Overspoiling them.
- Having codependent relationships with them.
- Surrounding yourself with lots of animals so that you feel more loved and that you are "good."

Know that your *extra*-loving, good intentions come from a huge loving heart that sincerely wants to help your animals be as happy and safe as they can be so that they will have a good life. Truly they are blessed to have you in their lives, as compared to someone who hasn't necessarily awakened to appreciate the gifts that can arrive through having a deeper emotional connection with animals.

The desire and good intentions to give more and more love to your pets is a direct reflection of your not having received enough love as a child.

Any form of overloving actions is typically run by your inner child, or the part of you that did not get your needs met when you were young. And these beautiful, furry, scaled, and winged souls are giving the inner child something it dearly longs for: love, acceptance, companionship, and even adoration.

You are also at a higher risk of overprotecting and over-loving your animals if you were overcontrolled as a child or experienced invasiveness. If a part of you has fears about feeling safe, it can be natural to want to overprotect your animals in a way you were not protected as a child.

Your inner child coming out to play with your animals and enjoying their company is wonderful for you and your pets. Animals help us stay young through play and exercise, and we all typically need to play more and have more fun; our beloved companions are perfect for fulfilling those inner needs.

They fill an emotional need as well because they are safe listeners and natural consolers, and we do not have any negative history with them to overcome. It would be wise, though, to raise your awareness and pivot to allow the more mature adult part of yourself to make the decisions around your pets' diet, healthcare, safety, and any big decisions on their behalf.

People who continue to accumulate more animal companions than they can afford or more than they can reasonably take care of indicates that their inner child is running the show; they are addicted to the love and attention they receive from the animals. However, no matter the number of animals they have, it will never be enough until these individuals fill themselves (their inner child) with the love that they seek externally from their pets.

Many times people with rescue animals overcompensate and overlove animals because they assume or know that they've had a difficult past. With good intentions, they think they need to fill a hole in their hearts and unknowingly spoil them. Your animal companion might then begin to exhibit negative behaviors that are rooted in your overloving, good intentions. They might exhibit separation anxiety, eating addictions, or even physical issues from fear-based s/mothering.

I've seen many bottle-fed dogs and cats that had a difficult first few weeks develop needy personalities or become quite overbearing and demanding from the extra coddling they are given by their human caretakers. Their birth mother, on the other hand, would never overnurture or spoil them, as her role is to naturally prepare them to take care of themselves and be independent.

It can be difficult to know the boundary line between caring for them and *over*loving them. There must be a certain level of healthy detachment for you to distinguish between the two. Finding your thoughts filled with trying to please them or being constantly focused on their perceived pain or their care is a sign that you need to pull your energy back a bit so you can see more clearly. They are blessed to have you in their lives, so be on the lookout for your own inner needs and patterns, and do the best you can. It will all work out for the highest and the best.

It's Never Enough:
Buddy's Story

One of my first clients, Kathy, hired me to do a session on her dog Buddy. I'll never forget walking into her dining room and seeing a pile of dog toys that reached literally to the ceiling. Kathy was quite proud of it and said everyone in the family had contributed to sending Buddy toys. Buddy also regularly received unhealthy food and treats, and he was obese.

Kathy believed that she was expressing her love for Buddy by buying toys and fancy beds for him and constantly giving him unhealthy treats. The reason Kathy reached out to me was because he had developed more aggressive behaviors with her and had even bitten her several times.

The behavior was created by her overloving, unhealthy actions on Buddy's behalf. She treated him like a king and was asking, "After all I've given him, this is the thanks I get?" Just like two-legged children, your animals will find a way to keep the giving and attention coming, especially for treat addictions. Those things really don't matter to the deeper relationship. His new negative behavior of aggression was mirroring to her how she treated herself, as well as the fact that she had unexpressed anger.

During his session, Buddy cleared a lot of Kathy's energy (anger, emotional pain, self-loathing, and sadness) that he had absorbed through the years. She had created the codependent relationship to fill a void and believed she needed Buddy's love to feel any sense of happiness. But ultimately it wasn't fulfilling for either of them because it was conditional *love.*

Until she began to look at developing healthy internal parenting skills and receiving healing for herself and Buddy, the odds were high that his behavior would continue. Kathy was not ready for inner healing at that time, so she ended up going to her veterinarian for assistance. Buddy was given Prozac daily, until he passed away several years later.

In a sense, this type of overgiving behavior from a person to their animals is an attempt to buy their love and loyalty. It comes from a strong need to be liked by one's pets, but it will never be enough no matter how many toys and treats they are given. Those types of needs are bottomless pits, and the animal will never be "full" because it cannot begin to fill what they are really needing, which is unconditional love and acceptance. Animals will benefit much more by developing healthy interactions, deeper emotional connections, and attention from their guardians through bonding time, play, and exercise.

The Codependent Relationship

"Animals are my life! I love animals more than people! I don't know what I'd do without my little Coco! He's my everything!"

Every love relationship goes through codependent phases and that's normal. However, you need to be on the lookout for any continual need in which you find yourself dependent on your animals for your happiness. You might have some inner needs not being filled that require your attention. Or perhaps you're aware that you're doing this, but haven't yet developed the healthy internal parenting skills needed to fulfill yourself. This can show up as an unhealthy clinginess with your pets or making extreme sacrifices to satisfy their needs over your own. There's an underlying need to be needed and appreciated (usually unconscious) that taps into your self-worth insofar as it's connected to and dependent upon your pet. The desire, conscious or unconscious, to have your animals express a needier, more conditional way of being with you—so that you can feel even more special from their love for you—is what creates an unhealthy, codependent relationship.

Sometimes what's behind the creation of these overly close-knit relationships is loneliness and a feeling of isolation or not being connected. The fastest way to resolve the feeling of loneliness is to connect spiritually to yourself and to a higher power. I believe every soul longs for and needs to feel truly fulfilled in the body, mind, *and soul* to experience the richest life possible.

Codependency with your animals can really show up when you start getting close to someone you're dating. Many people have indicated that their animals' like or dislike of someone they're dating is the barometer they use to determine whether or not they should continue seeing that person. Sometimes this technique is accurate, but it can be difficult to receive their message with clarity when in the middle of a codependent animal-human relationship. When codependency exists, the animal will not approve any person who takes away attention from their beloved person. When the person who was dependent on their animal for happiness shifts their codependency to the new person they are dating, their pet will be none too happy about it.

Three's a Crowd:
Murphy's Story

When Carrie met and fell in love with Ron, they couldn't have been happier. But Murphy, her terrier mix, didn't quite feel the same way. He was missing the overloving and nurturing he'd always received from his two-legged mama for three years. After Ron had moved in with Carrie, Murphy began acting out his anger and would urinate on Ron's clothing, pillow, or sometimes directly on him.

By the time they called me to schedule a healing session for Murphy, tensions were high and their household wasn't a happy one. Everyone seemed to be expressing anger in their own unique way. Carrie was even wondering if they'd have to find a new home for her beloved dog, though it would break her heart to do so. She had been giving him attention, but the inappropriate urination continued. This proved to be particularly difficult because she was falling in love with Ron. As such, she wanted to be feeling on top of the world, but Murphy's behavior was robbing the joy from her new relationship.

Ron was a good guy and really wanted to make his relationship with Carrie work as well, but Murphy's behavior was getting old fast.

Murphy also felt betrayed given that he'd always been the center of his mom's universe. He released a lot of anger during the session, both his anger and anger that he'd absorbed from Ron and Carrie. During the session, I observed Murphy beginning to allow more love in, which began to heal his betrayal wound.

After the session, I spoke with Carrie, who had been feeling guilty about Murphy's behavior potentially being her fault. We also discussed the importance of her releasing the guilt so she could more easily shift the relationship with her beloved dog to one that was healthy, rather than codependent. To release this guilt and heal her own abandonment wounds, Carrie decided to embark on her own inner healing journey and receive distance sessions to shift her self-talk in order that she could begin to love herself instead of constantly looking externally for happiness, love, and joy. Carrie loved the sessions, began meditating daily, and started feeling better than she ever had in her entire life.

As for Murphy, after his first session, I guided Carrie and Ron to focus their thoughts on the desired behavior and to give no attention to his negative behavior (as much as they could do this). I also encouraged the couple to thank Murphy for allowing Carrie to share her love in healthy ways with both Ron and Murphy. Carrie explained to Murphy her commitment to change their relationship so that it would be a healthier and more independent one, and assured him that there would always be enough unconditional love for him, too.

Murphy received three sessions over the next month to continue healing the emotional wound behind his behavior and to support the clearing of his codependent needs as well. During that month, even if he urinated somewhere inappropriately, which was occurring less frequently week by week, they continued to only praise him when he urinated outdoors and not focus on the undesired behavior.

Their relationship transformed into a healthier one, and the negative behavior completely stopped. Years later, Murphy is still doing very well and loves his new dad.

When you begin a new relationship, there's no need to give extra (guilt) attention to your animal companions. They will naturally and instinctively adapt to having a new person in your life if you are happy with that person. Sometimes when they act out, it's because you aren't listening to your intuition about the person you're in a relationship with, and they're showing you what you're really feeling on the inside.

And other times, as with Carrie and Murphy, your pet's actions will occur because there are abandonment wounds within you both that must be healed and released in order to transform your relationship with your pet—and your life.

Separation Anxiety

Years ago, I recall holding a friend's Chihuahua, who, when I walked a few feet from my friend, surprisingly began growling and baring his teeth at me. My friend then rushed over, swooped him up with pride and said with a smile, "Oh, he always does that because he can't bear to be away from me."

The core issue in the creation of separation anxiety is realizing that it's not only about the animal; it's also about the people they are in relationship with. When you are open to the possibility of seeing and knowing this as truth, the wheels will be set in motion to create a shift around this issue in your relationship with your animal.

Separation anxiety is rooted in an unhealed abandonment emotional wound in you both. Many rescue animals have separation anxiety from the day they arrive in their foster homes or their new homes. Even so, there are no coincidences with the vibration and issues of the animals that show up in your life, even if they are foster animals. There will be potential gifts in the experience, however short the amount of time that they spend under your care.

Destructive chewing, barking, obsessive licking, anxiety scratching, and inappropriate elimination are just a few of the behaviors that can show up when people leave their pets while working or when traveling. It can be frustrating for all involved. I've seen people crate their animals with up to three different locks to keep their pets from escaping and damaging something in the house when they're not home. It's important to stop focusing on the animal as being "bad" if you don't like its behavior, or "good" if you secretly enjoy the fact that your animal longs for you when you're apart. You might also be extremely focused on their anxiety and replay it over and over again in your mind.

Separation anxiety is created from your animal not having gotten the feeling of being full from its birth mother (see page 62 for more on the Needy One), which would have helped to create a more secure, individuated self with no need to seek out a codependent relationship. As the animal matures, the early lack of fulfillment shows up in a distorted belief that it can only get its needs met externally. However, no matter how much love, attention, and food you give your animal, it will never be enough. *More often than not, I've seen separation anxiety dramatically shift by people simply raising their awareness to one of self-empowerment and acting from a higher level of consciousness.* Coming from a more empowered sense of self is the first step to begin the healing needed within you both.

Another clue to confirm that you are a contributor to your animal's separation distress is if you feel guilty when you leave them because you know they will be upset, and/or you tend to overcompensate with your affections in an attempt to make up for being gone. While you are away, they will have all of their needs taken care of and will be just fine. Breathe that sentence in until you feel its truth in every fiber of your being. It's not as if you're leaving them in the wild to fend for themselves when you're not with them. In your mind, begin to see them as being more secure and independent, because they pick up on your thoughts and energy.

It's a gradual healing process for them to begin to recognize and believe in their own divinity so they will feel secure in and of themselves without the need to suck energy from their person to "survive." Understand that this is exactly what's happening when you allow them to continue this pattern, which can be draining for you because you must constantly give your pets energy that they do not yet have the ability to retain. Animals cannot take energy from you without your consent at some level. Most people, with good intentions, think that they are helping their animals by continuing to give them increasing amounts of attention and energy. This only helps to continue, and even worsens their separation anxiety, and can be extremely frustrating for you both.

If their behavior triggers anger within you, it could be you are projecting your anger from some other aspect of your life onto them. Every situation is different, but if you're only focusing on controlling and fixing the animals' behaviors, it will be a long, frustrating process.

Beautiful change can occur by being gentle with yourself and your animal and getting assistance where needed to heal the relationship from the inside out.

Basic Tips to Ease Separation Anxiety

1. Make an intention to come from a more grounded place of empowerment regarding their distress around being alone. Give yourself permission to disengage from the usual feelings it triggers within you and see it all from a higher perspective. Pulling back your energy will free up space for the Divine to be able to assist you with the desired transformation.

2. Leave them alone while you are at home for short periods of time every day so they can become more independent.

3. Prepare your animal for some alone time by burning off some energy before you leave. Maybe take them for a walk or engage in a few minutes of playtime.

4. Avoid tearful good-byes that might be feeding your ego and your codependency needs. In your thoughts and visualizations, see them feeling safe and having all of their

needs met. Assume they will be fine when you're not together.

5. While you're away, visualize your animal feeling safe, secure, and peaceful. Believe and know that they are fine, and if your thoughts go to fear around what your animal is doing, pivot gently to seeing them enjoying the alone time.

6. Quiet down the happy reunions by avoiding petting or greeting your animal until they settle down.

7. Resist reprimanding them or focusing on the negative behavior. Scolding them for something done while you are gone will only make things worse and cause more anxiety.

8. Give praise and gratitude to your animal for the slightest of positive changes. You both need and deserve compassion and love while healing the deeper emotional issues behind the separation anxiety.

Essential Wisdom

Animals will have fewer negative behaviors and feel better when you create a deep bond in healthy ways. They are blessed to be with you and know that your care and companionship, along with providing a safe and loving home filled with unconditional love, is what allows them to have meaningful and fun experiences.

Believe and know that they love you unconditionally just as you are. *Love them more than your need to be loved by them. Accept the beautiful gift of their authentic, pure love as being enough, and focus on filling any void within yourself with a heaping dose of self-love.*

7

Projection Happens

Psychological projection is a defensive action that some people subconsciously use to release emotions. It's a coping mechanism wherein the person is triggered by an unhealed emotional wound, like a betrayal, for example. When the original wound is triggered through an experience they think is also a betrayal, then the person may project their feelings and emotions onto the subject as if that being was the same being that inflicted the initial wound.

This means that animals can also become the subject of their person's projection, as in the following example of Liz and Miso. It is important to bring awareness around projection with your animals so the relationship can be salvaged and transformed.

Misguided Expression:
Miso's Story

Liz was very skeptical about my work, given that she was unfamiliar with healing through the energy field. Her mother had read an article about me in the local newspaper and thought she'd try one last thing before rehoming or possibly taking her cat Miso to the county shelter. Miso was urinating outside of the litter box in many places throughout her home. Liz had tried traditional methods and even anti-anxiety medications recommended by her veterinarian without success and found that his behavior was negatively affecting not only their relationship, but also her happiness in general.

During the session, I observed that Miso released a lot of Liz's anger that had been projected onto him about his behavior. Frequently, if there is no other physical issue, animals will use urination to express and release anger—most certainly they are telling you that something is up through their actions.

After Miso's session, I asked Liz if she might have any unexpressed anger in some aspect of her life at the time. I then heard a small gasp, and she began to cry. As it turned out she was very unhappy at work, specifically with her boss; most days she left work feeling a lot of pent-up anger. During her evening commute, she would think about how it would make her day even worse if she got home and found that Miso had urinated outside of the box—again. Once home and having found another area that had been soiled by Miso, she'd redirect the repressed (boss) anger (energetically) onto her beloved cat.

In that moment, Miso was the believed reason for her anger, but he was simply the vehicle with which to mirror her anger and help her to release it. Her boss was who she was really angry with. We talked about new ways for her to release her anger, for I sensed she was open-minded and ready to raise her awareness to the higher purpose of his actions.

Once Liz became more conscious of the fact that she was possibly projecting her anger onto her cat, the energy in the house completely shifted. Now, as soon as she gets home, Liz gets on her treadmill to move out the negative *energy accumulated from repressing it at work. Not once since Miso's session has he urinated outside of the litter box. Not. Once. Liz also noticed a positive change in Miso, in that he was more relaxed and happy from that day forward.*

Seeing the Big Picture:
Lucy's Story

Another client, Melissa, called me to arrange a healing session. Furious with her cat Lucy's negative behaviors, she had even given her the unfortunate nickname Bitch Kitty. From the beginning of our initial conversation, I knew there was some hefty projection happening because the cat's behaviors should not have created the level of emotion I was hearing from Melissa. The behaviors ranged from her cat jumping on the countertop to not being kind to her dog and getting into things in the barn that Melissa didn't want her to get into.

Melissa had received much abuse as a child from a perfectionist mother, and Melissa was projecting her repressed anger toward her mother onto her cat. She was very open to hearing about the bigger picture of what was happening.

In addition to facilitating a session on Melissa's cat, I highly recommended that Melissa revert to using Lucy's real name versus the negative nickname, as animals will embrace the energy associated with their name.

Rise above Your Projections
for Healing to Occur

In the stories above, both Liz and Melissa, after experiencing their cats' negative behavior, had been projecting their own unexpressed anger onto their pet. This caused them to tap into their own feelings of invasiveness, of not being respected, or feelings that they didn't matter or that they had been betrayed.

Once they both were able to see the situation from the higher perspective, they pivoted to healthier ways to move out their anger instead of redirecting it on another soul (their cats). Instead they could work on healing themselves. The cats' actions were mirroring the emotional energy they were feeling from their people.

It's simple: If your animal makes you angry, then you have anger that needs to be released. Typically, when a person is projecting onto their animal, how they treat their animal is a direct reflection of their inner dialogue or inner critic. Many animal abusers, whether they are committing small or large acts of abuse, are guilty of this shadow projection onto their animals.

> *Typically, when a person is projecting onto their animal, how they treat their animal is a direct reflection of their inner dialogue or inner critic.*

If you're in a situation where you feel a negative reaction to an animal's actions, you might just be projecting. Thus it would behoove you to look at ways to help you heal the triggered emotional wound within you. Step away from the situation and take a deep breath. Go for a walk, maybe scream into a pillow, but intend to release the emotions in a healthy way, and understand that the triggered emotions are definitely coming up for a reason . . . to be released! You will want to consciously avoid giving the emotions to someone else to carry, as this can hurt them emotionally, be painful to bear, and create negative karma.

Many times, how you treat your animals is how you *wish* you were treated as a child. There is almost a feeling of idolizing one's pets and putting them on a pedestal, worshipping them, and thinking they can do no wrong. Some people find their animals cute and funny and perfect no matter what they do or how they behave. This is projecting your golden light onto your pet.

These animals are carrying a very important part of you that you need to see when you look in the mirror. They are hoping you will see that the love and joy you see in them is actually a mirror for you. While it may appear that these animals are consciously very content with holding a beautiful part of yourself, at a soul level, it is out of balance for you both.

It's really your inner child that's in charge of the pets' care when golden-light projection is happening. Although sometimes that is fun, it goes hand-in-hand with a heightened fear of losing them. Underneath it all is the distorted belief that you'd be absolutely crushed and lost without your pet.

Here's the nugget for you in giving or projecting your golden light onto your animals: The positive, beautiful attributes you see in them are also in you. Your animals have complete clarity in seeing the divine spark of golden light that is you. You can honor them by beginning to believe you *are* what they see in you.

Essential Wisdom

When you become aware of projection with your animal, it instantly becomes a blessing. You're having a human experience, so be gentle with yourself. Your animals are stronger than you realize, forgiving, and they can release any absorbed energy much more quickly than people can. They are masters at living in the present moment instead of reliving the past or worrying about the future. Give yourself a break, with a heaping dose of compassion, as your awareness increases around your relationship. Your animals will feel that, too.

8

Perfection Is Overrated

What happens when the animal you excitedly brought home begins chewing the computer and digging up your favorite flowerbeds? Or consistently knocking over the garbage can or jumping up on the countertops and helping himself to your dinner?

Managing Expectations

High Expectations:
Bailey's Story

Years ago, I received a call from a new client, Judy. She'd just rescued an adult dog named Bailey. He was the first dog she'd had since childhood decades earlier. Judy was filled with excitement and enthusiasm about adopting a new dog and had the future all mapped out. She would take Bailey running with her, and they'd sit quietly by the fire on cold winter nights; the dog would ever so gently lay its cute nose on her lap and fall asleep like a good dog. They'd play together and engage in many outdoor activities.

When she told me all of this, I felt as though she were describing a Norman Rockwell painting. The purpose of her call was to stop behaviors she had a lot of anxiety about:

Bailey continually jumped up on the bed, no matter how many times she tried to get him to stay off of it, and he would also distract Judy and want to play with her when she worked at home. Judy had tried using a trainer unsuccessfully; since she preferred using holistic healing, she wanted to try healing Bailey by clearing his energy.

During our conversation, I could feel the frustration that Judy felt toward Bailey. "Where is the perfect dog I ordered from the universe?" was the feeling I got from her.

It can be surprising that your animal companion has emotional and physical wounds that need healing, but, again, that's why you are together. They are always mirrors, positive or negative, to help you to learn, grow, heal, and evolve.

In my discussions with Judy after Bailey's sessions, it was clear that Judy was a perfectionist, and my sense was that she was pretty hard on herself. When I would ask if she could relate to certain emotional wounds that I'd observed and sensed Bailey working on during his session, Judy would consistently state that she didn't have any unhealed emotional issues.

Many people were raised in households that labeled children and animals as good or bad, and parents tried to mold them into the perfect child or animal. Once they become adults and have animals of their own, however, this can contribute to their actions being rooted in perfectionism, since that was the behavior that their parents modeled for them.

Sometimes bringing an animal into a family that has high expectations for the perfect pet can shift everything for the better. They fall in love with the animal, and their preferences for having no animal hair on the counter and never allowing them to sleep on the bed are thrown out the window in the name of love. It's a wonderful thing to witness someone who was a perfectionist shift gears because an animal has opened their heart.

Sometimes, though, the relationship is just not meant to be, as with Bailey, who was rehomed into a much better environment for him. I'm certain, though, that their time together brought numerous gifts to both Bailey and Judy. Some people really like animals, but that doesn't always mean they will love and enjoy having an animal companion or allow in or even desire a deeper bond with animals.

This is why the better orphan-animal organizations conduct in-home visits before they release the animal to the new family. They've seen countless animals returned when people are unprepared for the animals having different personalities or behaviors than the family or person envisioned. The facility's staff will know the animal's personality and do everything possible to ensure that the fit is a good one designed to go the distance.

If you have returned an animal before, know that it was also the right decision at the time for all involved, or it wouldn't have played out the way it did. I've seen quite a few situations in which an animal exhibited dangerous behavior or maybe didn't get along with the other animals in the house. If it were meant to be, it would have worked out. Know that everything unfolds as it should for the highest and best of all.

Animals, like every other soul on the planet, are born with their own unique personalities and experiences that can create behaviors that at first seem intolerable. However, with love and patience, things can change for you both through your soul commitment to heal together and feel more love in your hearts.

With love and patience, things can change for you both through your soul commitment to heal together and feel more love in your hearts.

Essential Wisdom

When you can accept your animals just the way they are—for they know no other way to be than their authentic selves—then you will find it is much easier to accept all parts of yourself as well. Open yourself to your emotions—to feeling in ways you did not know were possible. The human experience can be richer and more satisfying when you're not repressing your emotions and protecting yourself from feeling pain.

What you don't feel, you don't know. It's impossible to repress only the negative emotions, because in protecting yourself from feeling these emotions you also prohibit yourself from feeling love, joy, compassion and gratitude more deeply, not to mention the feeling of being spiritually connected to all. Your emotions are a gift in every way possible and a compass for feeling better and living with more clarity and peace within. It takes courage to feel, but when you are able to open yourself, the relationship you have with your pet can blossom into a heart connection unlike any you may have had before. Now, that is divine perfection.

Animals, like us, are living souls. They are not things. They are not objects. Neither are they human. Yet they mourn. They love. They dance. They suffer. They know the peaks and chasms of being.

Gary Kowalski

PART FIVE
THE REASON

Love of animals is a universal impulse, a common ground on which all of us may meet. By loving and understanding animals, perhaps we humans shall come to understand each other.

DR. LOUIS J. CAMUTI

9

Higher Purpose

As a young child I remember lying in the grass in the backyard, watching massive flocks of starlings as they graced the sky in synchronicity as one beautifully orchestrated unit. I was mesmerized by how connected they were, and I imagined being one of them. It felt comforting and nurturing. Even back then, I was able to see the energy that was through and around them that I now know is an oversoul.

To this day, when I hear the calls of the sandhill cranes or Canadian geese migrating overhead, I excitedly watch with the glee of a child, still mesmerized by the fluidity and grace of such a sight. To be so divinely interconnected to a grander conscious whole is how we are all designed to be at our core. We long for the peace, for the trust, and for the ease that comes with that feeling and knowing we are all equal. We are all one.

All animals that live and travel in flocks, herds, packs, pods, schools, and the like have oversouls that keep them energetically connected with the higher purpose of meeting the needs of all. How beautiful a notion it is to think that even humans could hopefully evolve to that one day. Dream with me!

Animal lovers and protectors frequently get fired up about their desire to protect and serve those beings that do not have a human voice. However, in keeping with the ebb and flow of the starlings flying in unison in the sky, know that every situation is serving a higher divine purpose for the good of all.

Higher Purpose with Your Pets

Our relationships with the animals that come into our lives, however briefly, also serve a higher purpose, for we are connected at a soul level. Try reflecting back to an animal that has come and gone from your life and try to find the higher purpose of the relationship. Was it to teach you to love? How to play? How to heal or grieve? How to feel? Or to support you until you transitioned into a new chapter of your life?

Animals are evolving their souls just as we are, and we are all born with a higher purpose.

John the Wise Mule

When Jim's family adopted a mule, they had no idea the impact it would have on their family. The mule, John, became a family member and was in touch with a higher knowing as to what was needed within the family to help them heal and stay connected. When John was with the family, they all got along better.

After Jim's mother passed, John went to live with Jim's sister Shirley on her small farm. At this point, Jim and his siblings all seemed to go their own ways and did not stay in touch any longer. Years went by, and one day, John the mule somehow got out of his area and walked to the middle of the street in front of Shirley's house and wouldn't budge. Drivers honked at him and several people stopped in an attempt to move him, all to no avail. Finally, the police were called. They went door-to-door to find his owner. The police officers then found out that Shirley had passed away in her house just that morning, and it became crystal clear why John the mule had ventured out into the road and stood his ground.

John's higher gifts to the family continue to this day: Jim and his siblings reconnected through Shirley's passing. They also needed to determine where John would next live. After a long period of being estranged Jim and his siblings are closer than ever before. Their best family memories are made when John is at the center of them, for this is when they feel their love for each other the most. John is one wise mule and is a prime example of an animal who has and is serving a higher purpose.

The Higher Purpose in Animal Abuse

So what's the higher purpose for animals that are negatively affected by humans, as in what occurs with oil spills and dog-fighting, for instance?

If you're an animal lover, hearing stories of their suffering will no doubt bring up much emotion within you, from sadness to anger. If you feel these emotions, it's official: you've been loved unconditionally by an animal. Anyone who says you're overly sensitive simply can't relate to your reactions. (I'm a double Cancer, the most sensitive sign in the zodiac, so I might have been told I'm sensitive just a few times in the past!)

Animals are safe to love, which means we love them with our whole heart. Because of our wonderful experiences with our animal companions, we don't want to see any of them suffer. And as animal lovers, we frequently see them as defenseless beings without voices or protection.

*Animals are safe to love, which means
we love them with our whole heart.*

The desire to save an animal from a perceived negative situation can ignite a lot of sparks within animal lovers and sensitive souls with big hearts. The reactions range from not watching the news at all because it's too painful seeing the animals suffer, to watching and reading every story of animal suffering and responding with anger and then taking action.

Every single person has suffered in some way. That can contribute to why it hurts, as well as why animal lovers become enraged when they see animals that are suffering in some way. It might also cause people to overreact from their wounded selves. If you find your reactions are off the chart around a particular situation involving a suffering animal, you may be relating to the animal's situation in some way, and it's time to take a step back. It could have triggered a response fueled by a past (unhealed) wound in your life.

Know that you will feel better when you can get to the higher purpose, and then maybe you will feel drawn to act on the animal's behalf.

Living in the Atlanta area in 2007, I was exposed to constant media stories about the legal case involving Michael Vick, a former quarterback of the Atlanta Falcons. He had been involved with dogfighting rings. While a huge part of me was outraged by his cruel participatory behavior, I also noted the fabulous gift the case proffered by shedding light on dogfighting nationwide, perhaps even globally. Suddenly, it was politically correct for dogfighting rings to be exposed and shut down.

New laws were put in place to deal with criminals, and

Michael Vick seemed to be the poster child to carry the weight of all those who have ever abused a dog. Thousands upon thousands of people were moved to take action to stop dogfighting in a way that would not have happened otherwise and in part, as a result, Congress passed the Animal Fighting Prohibition Enforcement Act of 2007. Innumerable dogs' lives were saved that year, and people lined up in droves to help them.

It was similar with the Exxon Valdez tanker oil spill in 1989 and the BP oil spill in the Gulf of Mexico in 2010. The animals that sacrificed their lives were not lost in vain, for their struggles served a higher purpose of bringing out compassion from mankind on their behalf. This led to new guidelines and the development of new methodologies that prevented oil spills from reoccurring in the future.

The Higher Purpose of Wild Animals That Connect with People

Many times I've seen animals from the wild break out of their typical environment and allow themselves to be loved by a human. It takes much courage and desire, driven from the higher life purpose and intentions of the animals, to leave the kinship of their species and get closer to humans. However, this is one of the fastest ways they can evolve their souls.

I know it's hard for many to think of dolphins, big cats, elephants, or any animal known to typically live in the wild to be in a life other than that of their natural habitat. The freedom fighters within all of us want to open every cage door and let all the animals free. Certainly, when there is mistreatment of an animal, appropriate action to help them is needed. But frequently the animals want to be with people to evolve and grow in a way they would not be able to in their own natural environments.

A human's love and interaction raises their vibration and level of consciousness so they can serve at a higher level. Some of them are not ready to have that experience, so it's important for us humans to honor their desires. Frequently, if an animal is in touch with people, it is because they are serving as a teacher of their species to raise awareness.

> *A human's love and interaction raises animals' levels of consciousness so they can serve at a higher level.*

Raise your vibration around the situation and see them as teachers and guides. Thank them for their service and send them love. They will feel your higher vibration, and that in and of itself is a gift and blessing to them.

The Higher Purpose of Working Animals

Many animals love giving back and serving people, as it fills their heart with joy and purpose (read more about these master healers in chapter 5). We all know of service dogs and farm animals who work to serve people and be part of a higher purpose. I've found especially with dogs, but also with other species like horses and cats, that it's important to give animals a job or purpose so that they can serve the family and have a sense of responsibility. A few examples might be for them to greet everyone with love, to help take care of another animal or child in the house that could have physical limitations, or to teach the children patience and compassion.

Roy the Carriage Horse:
Shouldering Joy

While coordinating a Healing Touch for Animals® work-shop at Save the Horses animal rescue center in Cumming, Georgia, I connected energetically with a retired carriage horse whose shoulders had seen better days. This incredible horse was given freedom to roam the entire rescue farm, and I got the feeling he was a very wise, grounded, old soul who held space for all of the animals and people visiting, living, and/or volunteering at this progressive animal rescue organization.

While connected with him, I could feel the tremendous joy he'd had serving as a carriage horse and how much he enjoyed bringing smiles to everyone who rode in the carriage. Yes, his shoulders were sore, but he had served a higher purpose of his soul's choosing. Roy lived to be forty years young and left a legacy of love to many people and children. He was a master of bringing light and love to people.

Just as people who have an area of their body that is tired as a result of work, animals might as well. For example, a farmer who loves farming may not want to retire just because his body has aches and pains. And we've all heard about people who lost their love of life when they retired. Animals can be similar in that their joy-filled purpose out-weighs any physical discomfort they may experience "on the job."

Though Roy's carriage-pulling days were behind him, it was not enough for him to simply be in the pasture day in and day out like many thought he should be in his elder years. He wanted to be part of greeting and wel-coming all visitors to the ranch so that he could continue serving others.

Animals, like people, have positive and negative experiences that evolve their soul. And, as you already know because you're an animal lover, they love serving their people. However, they don't limit their service work to only people; they will also intentionally help another animal. Sometimes they will serve others at all costs, seemingly driven by a higher and more divine purpose.

One of the most impactful and powerful stories I can recall is about a rescued mama dog named Marty, her love story, and one of her puppies named 5Star.

A Bright Star:
5Star's Story

Gigi Graves, the founder of Our Pal's Place in Marietta, Georgia, contacted me about a new arrival, Marty, and her eight puppies, who had been newly birthed after arriving at the center. Marty had been diagnosed with pneumonia and was not doing well. Gigi asked if I could do an emergency session on her to expedite her healing.

During the session, Marty showed me that her heart was broken, which was the emotional wound behind the pneumonia. Marty shared how she had lived on the streets with a male dog who had sacrificed his life by running out in front of a car so that she could be caught and have a better life—not only for herself but for her puppies who were about to be birthed. She wouldn't leave his side as he lay in the street. Animal control was contacted, and Marty began a new life at Our Pal's Place where she gave birth to eight puppies within days of her arrival.

Marty released a lot of grief during her session, but afterward she was still in pretty bad shape from everything she had gone through. Gigi had to make the very difficult decision to separate her from the puppies so she could be treated with medication to enhance her chances of survival. I felt very positive about Marty's desire to live from what I sensed during her session.

Marty was a very caring and gentle mother to her puppies even while ill and was none too happy about being separated from them. The good news is her body quickly and positively responded to the medications.

Unfortunately, we then had to switch gears and turn our attention to the pups, all of whom now had life-threatening respiratory infections passed down from their mom—some worse than others. All eight of them had to be bottle-fed.

Due to the extreme nature of the infection, even with the best of care, three of the pups perished within days. Their tiny two-week-old systems were just not developed enough to fight it off.

Then there were five.

5Star was the next critical case and needed an emergency energy healing session. During the first session I did with her, I was surprised to feel the four surviving puppies energetically connected to and taking energy from 5Star. My logical mind immediately went to thoughts of animals in the wild and how, in packs, the weak one is sometimes pushed out. But I was quickly corrected by 5Star as I received information that she wanted to do this for them—it was part of clearing her karma and evolving her soul and it was the reason why she was with them. She wanted to help them get stronger and move forward to have a good life.

5Star responded so positively to the session that we all cheered and were very hopeful. She began taking the bottle on her own; and Gigi no longer had to force-feed her. But a couple of days later, that changed as she went downhill *again. Another session still showed the darkness in her lungs and energy going to her siblings. For the next twelve hours, either Gigi or her husband Jeff cradled 5Star on top of their hearts in hopes that the love and direct contact could breathe new life into her lungs.*

She transitioned in the middle of that night, knowing utterly and completely the unconditional love of her birth mother and her caretakers as well. She was a teacher for us all in many ways. I am so grateful for knowing this amazing soul who gave her life so her siblings could all live on and be adopted into wonderful homes. Mama Marty also went on to be adopted by a loving home whose family helped her to heal from her losses so she could have an easier, joy filled life.

There is always a divine plan, and when you raise your level of consciousness to begin to believe there is a higher purpose in every situation, it can help you understand, why perceived "bad" things happen.

Whenever you feel emotionally triggered by an event involving an animal, try stepping back from it to see what the higher purpose of it might be. This will help you to raise your vibration so you can feel better. Once you feel better, you will be able to discern the entire turn of events more clearly.

And remember, every animal situation is unique. My intention is to merely point out that there might be another way to look at each situation you encounter with animals. This may help you understand why the animal came into your life and if there is a higher plan and purpose that is intended to be a springboard for positive growth and change.

Check in with your heart after experiencing an initial reaction to a story of animal suffering. You might be relating at some level to the animals' *perceived* suffering. Utilize that message and its accompanying gift for your own inner healing and then decide if you want to take divinely guided action on that animal's behalf.

I've seen so many touching stories of people who saw starving horses in a field and, instead of judging the owners, they instead approached them with compassion and a desire to help. In turn, they were privy to amazing, gut-wrenching stories, which then prompted kind, heart-centered outreach efforts for all involved. The rule of thumb is to be the person you want the perceived abuser to be.

Animals have been tremendous teachers for mankind and had the brave ones not chosen, at a soul level, to courageously leave their family in the wild to serve humans, we would not have evolved as quickly as we have. I recommend the following acknowledgment of their gifts to us, to amplify the good feelings that such gratitude engenders.

Place your hand gently on your heart and send gratitude and love to all animals. Thank them for their courage, knowledge, love, teachings, and service to our planet, and for serving a higher purpose—each and every day.

Essential Wisdom

There are endless gifts waiting to be revealed in your relationships with animals. Reach for the higher purpose in every experience, for in the center of every situation and experience is where you will find the Divine orchestrating every detail.

In cases of animal abuse, sometimes the animal is not suffering as much as you might think. Sometimes they are. What's important is for you to get grounded and move out of a heightened state of emotion in a healthy manner before you take action. Cry, scream into a pillow, exercise, but go with the flow of the emotions that are coming up. They're being revealed because they hold gifts for you upon their healthy release.

It's preferable that your decisions and actions come from your adult self in these types of situations, so love yourself in spite of the emotions that are arising. Good internal parenting filled with compassion and kindness will help to clear and heal the emotional wounds rather than just circulating the energy. This allows you to observe your emotions with empathy but detach from relating to what you see. You might need to disconnect from reading or watching so many stories about animal abuse or suffering until you can get grounded. You may also want to receive help from a healing practitioner.

Marty on the day she was united with her four surviving pups.

❖═══════ ✳ ═══════❖

Change the way you see things, and the things you see will change.

WAYNE DYER

PART SIX

THE WAY

The love of all living creatures is the most noble attribute of man.

CHARLES DARWIN

10

Big Decisions

The big decisions are inevitable and rarely easy to make.

- Should I rehome my dog? He's bitten my toddler twice, and we have a baby on the way!
- My cat was just diagnosed with cancer; should we do the treatments my vet says might give him a lot more time or help him transition?
- I'm ready for a new dog—which one is the right one?

My intention in this chapter is to help you realize that keeping your power in every decision is necessary for your growth and for making better, clearer choices on your animals' behalf. Trusting yourself when you're stressed out or when you face the potential loss of a beloved companion can feel overwhelming and scary. Seeing your companions in pain and suffering can really get you ungrounded, in which case it's very hard to be clear.

There are no exceptions; everyone is having a very human experience. So when you're in the middle of a big decision about your animal, it can be natural to look externally for the answers. Let's face it: we're all so programmed to give away our power in those moments to another person. We just want the problem solved and long for someone else to fix it.

Think about it. We were all taught, when making big decisions, to give away our power from a young age. For instance, what happens when you go to a doctor? It's a step-by-step process:

1. What's wrong?
2. Fix it!
3. Tell me what to do, when to follow up, and what medications to take.

We're programmed to trust those individuals who we believe to be more knowledgeable than we are. Healing practitioners do serve an amazing purpose, and I highly encourage creating a team of those you can rely on and trust to *partner* with you to help you determine the best course of action you can take when making a major decision about your animal(s).

The Power Derived from Looking Within

The subconscious desire to let someone else tell you what to do is created to avoid the potential pain you perceive you might feel (if you make the "wrong" choice) or might cause your beloved animal. This avoidance actually prevents you from tapping into your inner wisdom, which is the land of golden clarity and it holds the key to knowing the highest and best path for your beloved animals. Yes, it takes courage and intention to cultivate and then listen to your inner guidance, but doing so will help you mature and grow, and you will learn to trust yourself.

Take a deep breath and really take this in: No one knows your animals better than you. No one.

No one knows your animals
better than you.

Our fears of causing our animals any type of suffering or pain or even of losing them brings us to a place I call Crazy-Fix-It-Island (CFII)—a place I've been to frequently, I might add. Know that when you're visiting CFII, the unconscious belief is simply this: "I won't be able to handle the pain if _____ happens to my little Tobey. It will be too much for me, so I have to fix him and fast."

This reaction is completely normal. Indeed you *are* their guardian and responsible for their care. While visiting CFII, you will justify your actions and stay in busy mode to avoid facing (and releasing) your fears. Let's look at fear in general. Think about how many crazy fears you've had that never came true. Good stuff gets through to you despite them. Think of your fears as simply unhealed emotional wounds coming up to clear. Then intend to go within to more intimately get in touch with yourself and your inner knowing. It's an inside job.

As you can imagine, I receive many inquiries asking if I can determine if an animal is ready to transition or if the person should try everything they can to help them heal. This is a big decision that most all animal lovers will find themselves in, including myself. This life-or-death decision we sometimes must make on behalf of these beautiful souls who have graced our lives is nothing short of being one of the most, if not *the* most, difficult decisions we will ever make.

Here is one example from my own life showing how I learned to keep my decision-making power when it came to the care of my animal companions.

Learning to Trust Myself:
MaiTai Guy

Twelve years ago, my now seventeen-year-old cat MaiTai was having quite a few physical issues, and I felt helpless and very scared. I'd lost three companions a couple of years prior, which was all too fresh on my heart. I was worried about him, and my worst fears haunted me. I decided to contact an animal communicator I'd recently met. She'd seemed so connected, and I desperately wanted help as to what MaiTai wanted me to do.

When the animal communicator returned my call, I simply asked if she had any information about all of his physical issues, and without hesitation or asking more details she said, "It's his time." Just like that. "It's his time." I sat there in shock, disbelief, and utter horror. I hung up the phone and began crying. All night long I tossed and turned, didn't sleep at all, and was a total mess as I began grieving yet another loss.

Over the next couple of days, I began to rethink what she'd said, and on some level realized I'd given her my power. An inner knowing began surfacing that told me to hold off on making any big decisions. It's easy for me to reflect and see how that experience was an extraordinary lesson on how people with intuitive gifts can slip into their egos during a client's vulnerable time and imagine they have all the answers. It was a tough lesson learned, and a painful one, but it made me very clear about the fact that it was not his time.

A few days after my phone conversation with her, she called and frantically asked if I'd taken MaiTai to help him transition, and I firmly said no. Before I could continue, she began stating that she wasn't so sure it was his time after all. Apparently, she'd told another recent client the same thing, and when they took their dog to the vet, he fought and fought and fought as if it wasn't his time right up until he took his last breath.

Upon hanging up, I was tearful again, thinking that if I'd given my power away to her, I wouldn't have my beloved cat who is still with me twelve years later. One of the many gifts from that interaction was helping me release grief from my previous animals' losses, which I sorely needed to do.

I honor the courage it took for her to call me back and hope she received gifts from the experience as well. I vowed to never play God with my clients when they were in the middle of making their big decisions. My role is to be a guide to help them rely on their deeper connection and inner knowing, which ultimately holds more gifts for both of them. It is my job as a healer to show people how to retain their own power and trust their inner knowing, not to tell them what to do so they become dependent on me.

Prior to that experience with MaiTai, I had another well-regarded animal communicator state that my cat Sundance would not be long for this Earth, and to be prepared that she would pass young. Her words haunted my thoughts until Sundance was at least eight or so years old (she's now sixteen).

Many people have shared positive experiences about animal communicators. Just listen to your gut. If something feels off, it is. As with any profession, there are good practitioners and some still finding their way. Even these experiences of mine bestowed immeasurable gifts upon me and helped me to clarify the lines of integrity and to keep my own power.

Following are *three steps* to catapult you out of the land of ambiguity so you will have clarity when making big decisions on behalf of your animal companion.

1. Help from a Higher Power

This one act can help more than all the others combined. It will remind you that you're not in this alone and that there are indeed spiritual resources to help you with any and all decisions. Time and time again, I've heard clients' stories of miraculous shifts when they asked for help from God, angels, or whomever they resonate with in a higher realm.

When you rely solely on the physical world to get you through tough times and big decisions on behalf of your animal, it limits the potential for less suffering for you both.

Many years ago, my cat MaiTai had gotten into a cupboard and then jumped through a small hole in the side wall of it and was trapped in a tiny area between two cupboards, and for whatever reason he was unable to jump back through the hole. He frantically tried for hours, and I tried everything I could think of to help him gain traction to get back out, all to no avail. We were both stressed out. I paced around the house, talking out loud, and thinking, *What will I do? Call the fire department?* Finally, I remembered my go-to question when I'm feeling helpless in a situation with one of my animal companions—*What would I tell my client to do in this situation?* Immediately I called upon God and the strength of Archangel Michael to help MaiTai get out of the walls inside of the cabinets, and within seconds he had easily jumped through the hole and walked over to me. Sometimes, we just need to get out of our own way so help may arrive.

You might also find that spirit speaks through a friend, family member, or practitioner during times of need. You will know when the guidance is coming from spirit, through the person, because it will resonate in your heart to be truth for you. If you are praying or asking for help and guidance, always ask for the highest and best outcome for your animal to occur and try, as much as possible, to be unattached to any specific outcome. This keeps the situation string-free for God to navigate through the heart of the matter.

Believing in a higher power is up to you, of course, but if you do, you'll find it's a resource like no other. To trust and have faith that you are being universally supported will bring you relief and allow grace to be the center of your big decision.

> *When you rely solely on the physical world to get you through tough times, it limits the potential for less suffering for you both.*

2. Surrender the Outcome

Let me be clear up front: surrendering the outcome doesn't necessarily mean that you shouldn't take action. It simply means to release what you think *has* to happen so what really *needs* to happen can reveal itself. It's difficult when we're so attached to our animals to not be invested in the outcome, but it's worth the effort to shift your energy. Once you release the need for the outcome to be a particular way, other options to help you with your big decision will appear, which could be even better than you imagined possible.

It's normal for people to think they have the answers, dig their heels in, and try many different ways to achieve their desired outcome. I recall when my client Mary was looking for a new place to board her horse, and she was adamant that one place was the answer because it had so many of the qualities on her list. She was on a mission, and while the new place presented one challenge after another, she kept pushing to make it work. Finally, I recommended letting go of the outcome, and after much resistance, she did—and an even better situation occurred, offering perks and benefits not even on her list, for less money per month.

Samantha, a long-term client, was ready for her next canine companion and frantically searched for a rescue dog online for many hours every day. Time after time, Samantha got emotionally invested in a particular dog, only to be disappointed because they ended up going to another home. Finally, with a little love coaching, she was able to pull back her energy and surrender into the process so that her beautiful new companion could arrive.

Everything will be easy and matters will come together quickly when it's the right and perfect companion. You will not have to charge into the situation thinking it's a competition or race. The companions that grace your life are divinely orchestrated appointments that you will not miss.

Try not to let fear fuel the choices you make in big decisions as it's counterproductive to attempt to control the outcome. Make a conscious intention to pull back your energy from your companions *and* from a particular outcome for whatever the situation is, and an easier process will unfold for you both.

> *The companions that grace your life*
> *are divinely orchestrated appointments*
> *that you will not miss.*

3. Heads-Up

You'll be surprised at the unique and creative ways that answers to your questions are trying to find you. In every situation where there is uncertainty in the choice you make and you have asked for guidance, help, or signs, be awake and aware of your surroundings and coincidences that could hold key answers to your questions. There might be someone who calls you out of the blue who holds the nugget of truth you needed to hear. You might receive answers in your dreams or through symbolism in the world around you. Maybe you'll notice a bumper sticker or sign along the road with a message. Nature can be one of the clearest channels from which to receive symbolic messages to help you with your decision. There are many websites and books to assist in clarifying specific interpretations from nature and animals in the wild. I'm most drawn to the books by (the late) Ted Andrews, but follow your guidance as to what's right for you. Once I had awakened to receiving messages through nature, I noticed there were hidden treasures everywhere to help me make the best decisions. I quickly came to rely on this resource that the universe had easily provided on my behalf.

Your animal companion could also be the one giving you the messages. For instance, if you are on the fence about whether or not your animal would like assistance in their transition, one of the signs might be that no matter what form of medical assistance you give, the situation doesn't get better or a new physical symptom shows up right after the other one has healed. When your animal companion is ready to go and you have integrated the gifts they have brought to you, their bodies will continue to manifest a means to release.

There have been very direct signs from my animals every time I've had to make that decision on their behalf. Sometimes they were very obvious signs, like with my cat Bailey. His quality of life had greatly deteriorated to the point that he hardly stood up much—yet I still questioned the decision to put him down. One evening I sat on the bed next to him and asked if he wanted me to help him transition.

Somehow he found strength—unlike any I'd seen in weeks—to get up and easily walk over to me and give me a big slurp on the cheek. Then he turned around and got back in his bed. Never again did I see that level of strength in him. In that moment, I knew he had given me permission to help him transition.

There are endless stories of animals giving their guardians obvious signs to help them make a decision on their behalf. Once they are able to release their fears, their human companion is able to observe the situation from a higher perspective. The animals that want to live every day until their bodies naturally release will be with people that want the same thing for them. Thus will every turn of events be divinely orchestrated.

Essential Wisdom

There is divine order and timing present in the middle of every decision you make on your animals' behalf. Go within yourself first for answers to the questions that are plaguing you. Hold on to your decision-making power and make a choice that you know in your heart is right, and if it's not clear, wait until it is. Everything will unfold just as it should.

11

Easing through Change

Moves . . . new family members . . . losses . . . divorce. It's not a matter of *if* there will be changes—it's *when*. Animals sense and feel the stress and emotions from their people, which show up when there are changes within the family and the home.

Overall, animals typically adapt more easily than people do to change and loss, but your energy is so enmeshed that they will want to help you feel better during difficult times. If they're unsure what is happening, they may have a heightened level of stress about the changes. I've found when people are worried about how their pets will adapt to change, their concern is typically just as much, if not more, about how exactly the change will impact *them*.

When I recently downsized and moved house, I was stressed out about having to go out of town just days after my cats and I had moved into the new place. I was certain my cats would think I'd abandoned them in this strange new place. In those first few days, they were hardly eating or sleeping and they were constantly roaming the house. But off I went, and my yoga instructor friend cared for them while I was away.

Upon arriving back home, I found two very settled and peaceful cats completely fine with their new surroundings. That's when I realized that I was the one who was worried about adjusting to the new place, not them. They were fine. They were mirroring me and feeling my redirected stress on them before I left. Once I'd gotten out of the house, they were able to settle in and get comfortable.

> *I've found when people are worried about how their pets will adapt to change, their concern is typically just as much, if not more, about how exactly the change will impact them.*

It's natural to want to help your animal companions ease through changes, so I want you to give them the permission and the space to adjust on their own as much as possible. Their natural adaptive instincts are superbly better than ours. When you work through your stress and as much as possible try not to worry about them, it will help *them* adapt more easily.

All beings go through change and difficult times. Without it, people and animals would not grow and evolve. Think about all of the changes and loss you have been through. While I'm certain much of it was not easy, you survived and are better for it. There are amazing gifts that arrive with the changes and losses all beings experience.

Following, I will address a few common changes that frequently occur.

Grieving a Loss

Yes, animals do indeed grieve. Be it a two-legged or four-legged friend they've lost, or when taken away from their birth mother and siblings, they will grieve the loss. You might see them sleeping in the bed of the pet that has passed. Sometimes they stop eating or seem depressed—sleeping more and not playing as much. They might not want to do their favorite things. Perhaps they have new short-term behavioral issues like chewing inappropriate things or urinating in inappropriate places.

The grieving process for animals is very individual and can last from a few days up to a year. On average, my observation is that animals grieve for two to three months. While it is difficult to witness them mourning, try as much as possible to allow them to grieve and move through the emotions in their own timing. They will get through it, just like you will.

Or grieve together. You might both want to sit on a blanket of the lost one and release some of your pain. It helps to talk it out with them—they will understand you on some level. Tell them, "Yes, I miss them too." If you have two-legged children, include them and let them see you grieve as well. It's healthy to model being human and feeling and releasing pain. It's a part of life, and when all of your children, two- *and* four-legged, are honored and respected via your giving them the space and timing they need to work through their grief, they will not be forced to repress their pain just because doing so makes you feel better.

When you honor their pace and the ways they choose to get through and process their grief, you honor yours as well. Resist going to Crazy-Fix-It-Island and know that you will all be fine by sinking into the process with the intention to *feel* your way through it. Detached compassion for them still allows love to flow between you both but keeps your fears at bay. It's a faster healing process when you open your emotional pipes and grieve alongside your animal companion.

Many people think they shouldn't cry around their animals because it'll stress them out. However, as stated earlier, *Your animals will absorb more of the emotions you repress as opposed to those you release.* It helps them more if you are not avoiding your grieving process.

Leave out a few objects with the scent of the person or pet to help them process the change more easily. Give them unconditional love and tell them that you are there for them and ask them to let you know what their needs are. That will give them the message—*I'm unattached to the outcome of the timing of your grieving process, and I am here for you.* Energy work is also quite beneficial for grieving, as it honors the soul receiving the session to help them release what they are ready to.

Know that they are so highly intuitive they might also give you signs that they see the soul of the one that passed or even act for an instant *like* the pet that has transitioned—as if they are suddenly a host for the pet that passed to pop in and say hello. These are very special heart-opening moments, so keep your eyes peeled for these treasured gifts.

Adding Another Pet to the Family

When you're ready to bring another animal into the house, it's important to let the existing animals be part of the decision. Trust me on this one: If you don't ask the current pets' permission or discuss the matter with them up front, it can backfire by the animals not getting along. I've heard some pretty severe situations that could have easily been avoided by including the animals of the household in the process. Consistently, I've seen more positive outcomes when people include their current animal companions in the entire process of taking in a new companion (two- or four-legged).

When we speak to them, I'm uncertain if they understand our exact words, but I know they read and feel our energy and receive the corresponding visuals in our minds. If you've recently had an animal that transitioned, you can also ask him or her to assist you from the other side. They love serving you!

When you ask your animal permission to potentially bring another animal into the house, if, for example, they turn and walk out of the room, that's a sign they're not ready yet. You might also get a sense from them if you just tune in to them with the question on your mind.

If you've already brought a new pet into the household unannounced, and the new pet isn't getting along with your animals or there's a new negative behavior, I highly recommend sitting down and apologizing to your companion about not asking their permission and promising you will always do that in the future. This will also help to release your guilt about the situation, and the energy will be cleared to enable a shift in the house.

Family Frustration:
Granger's Story

My client Nancy was at her wit's end when the new puppy she and her husband brought into the home sent their other dog, Granger, into a frenzy. Granger was urinating everywhere and shredding one of their chairs. They tried numerous potential solutions, which included bringing in a trainer and talking to the vet, who suggested Prozac for Granger, but nothing worked. They were worried they'd have to rehome one of their beloved dogs and wanted to try an energy healing session to see if it would help.

Once I connected with Granger energetically, I observed there was much anger being released and a feeling of being disrespected. The session cleared out a lot of his negative emotions and rebalanced him energetically. I then guided the couple to sincerely *(the animals will know if it's lip service) apologize to Granger about not including him in the decision to add the puppy to their family and promise to never do this again.*

A week or two after I facilitated the session, Nancy e-mailed to share the good news that Granger's negative behaviors had completely stopped the moment they'd apologized. They said they felt like they had their dog back again.

Moving to a New Home

Moving to a new home is one of the most stressful things people can go through. Many worry about their animals adjusting, especially if they know up front the new home will bring changes to their animals' routine and playtime.

In most new home situations, the animals will adjust just fine as soon as you assure them you'll still be together.

When you know where you are moving to, begin giving them verbal and visual images about the new place. Tell them about the positive qualities of their new home: where their bed will go, the bright window they will be able to look out of, or the sunny place in the house where they can nap.

There's no need to hide the situation from them in hopes it will stress them out less. They'll already know a big change or something is happening from your energy, so it's best to tell them as soon as possible and clear the air. Again, these conversations are great tools that allow you to shift your energy from worrying about them to *knowing* they will be okay. The wrong thing to do is to hide the truth to protect them, which keeps the energy in fear—and they can literally smell fear.

I've given similar advice to clients for many years and have been hearing from them how utilizing this advice made such a positive difference. I recall one client in particular who had the "moving conversation" with her cat, Simon. He was sitting on her lap, looking at her, and listening intently to her telling him about the upcoming move. Then he jumped down and walked over to his very favorite toy in the whole world and sat down next to it. Then Simon looked back to her, as if to say, "Okay, but is this toy coming with us too?" She laughed and told him absolutely they would be bringing his toys, beds, and all of his stuff. He then jumped back up on her lap and peacefully lay down and went to sleep.

Essential Wisdom

Through the changes in your life that can also affect your animals, make sure they have a good healthy diet and daily movement to help them more easily release the energy that the experience is creating. There are many holistic options that could help them through life's shifts and changes, such as pheromone plug-ins, essential oils, probiotics, and energy healing of course.

When you meditate, bring them into your thoughts (if they don't want to sit with you). The energy that flows through you while meditating will be very beneficial for you both as together you undergo the changes life is sure to send your way.

12

Imagining the Positive

Did you know that animals can not only feel your emotions, but they also see your mental images? This is how they know when you're coming home before you pull in the driveway or that you're going on a trip before you pull out the suitcase. All animal lovers have had many experiences that convince them their pet is either the smartest animal in the world or they're psychic!

Once you understand the power of your thoughts and begin to consciously control the visualizations you send your animal, you have created one of the most powerful tools possible to help your animals through changes, to aid in their healing, and especially in shifting their negative behaviors.

A Clean Slate:
Brady's Story

Earlier this year I received a call from a new client, Lynne, asking for help with her cat Brady, whom she'd rescued years ago from living under a house. Brady had always had an unfortunate habit of charging Lynne while she sat and would bite her arms to the point of drawing blood. I could feel her fear and anger as she spoke about the situation.

Lynn had tried many suggested methods and treat-

ments over the years from animal practitioners but none had changed his behavior, and she was at that "I'm over it!" place. She had tolerated Brady's behavior for a long time because she had a big heart and really hoped and wanted him to live a happy, safe life, but she was at her wit's end. That said, Lynne sincerely wanted him to be able to allow more love into his life.

When I worked on Brady I could see that he'd had a frightening past and certainly had anger locked in his energy field that he needed help with clearing. The other part of the shift that needed to happen pertained to the mental images Lynne was sending him. It's natural to consistently focus on the animal's negative behavior. You will replay it over and over again in your thoughts—thinking about how it annoys you, how you can get them to stop, or fearing they are doing it while you're gone, and, in turn, being angry or upset with them about it. It becomes a broken record that you can't get out of your head, and the more you focus on it, the worse it seems.

Here's the kicker: When they see the thoughts in your mind, they don't get the red circle with the line through it indicating that they should stop the behavior. They become confused because your thoughts are constantly focused on a particular negative behavior, which reinforces that behavior for them and in them, instead of having the opposite effect. So they repeat the behavior and it elicits a negative reaction from you, and the cycle continues, locked into a never-ending spiral that makes you both crazy.

After Brady's first session, I guided Lynne to wipe the slate clean in her mind and change the energy of expectation to the behavior she wanted to see from him. And, if she were to notice her thoughts returning to the negative behavior, to gently pivot and return to images of him being kind, gentle, *loving, and peaceful. I suggested that with each positive step Brady exhibited, no matter how small the action, that she increase the praise and send him love and gratitude for the desired behavior. I advised that she tell him how proud she was of his allowing more love into his life. The more praise the merrier, even if he was calmly and kindly sitting and looking at her.*

It was at least a month or two later when I next heard from Lynne, and it was to let me know that Brady had become more loving than she'd ever seen him and not once had he tried to bite her since his session. She was beyond thrilled that Brady had made such a turn for the positive, and she was being careful to send him only positive thoughts, images, and high praise for being more loving.

This tool of shifting your mental images to positive thoughts is necessary when trying to stop a negative behavior in your animal. The more you think about your animal's negative behavior, the more likely it is that they will continue the behavior. What you focus on expands, so change the energy of expectation to the behavior you desire. Make up a little movie if necessary to keep your thoughts in a positive place.

For example: Visualize your dog resting peacefully in the other room when typically he is begging for food at the dinner table. See yourself then giving him praise afterward, and his reaction of excitement and joy to receive such a positive reaction from you. Repeat.

Intentionally focusing on the behavior you desire your animal to have sends them a positive message and wonderful energy along with it. And you get a perk too. You feel better because it shifts your energy and gets you out of the reaction the behavior is triggering within you.

Maintain a Positive Focus
When You Travel

We've all gotten "the look" from our animal companions when we pull out the suitcase. Then the guilt arrives, and we begin apologizing for leaving them, assuming they will be devastated without us. Our minds begin to generate mental images of them not eating and perhaps tearing up furniture or urinating inappropriately. If this sounds familiar the reality is that, consciously or unconsciously, you ego wants to be missed and your psyche has inadvertently set up a need to be needed from them. Once you are able to acknowledge that the codependency dance takes two to tango, you can actually help your pets have an easier time while you're away. (See more in "The Love Bind.") Changing your expectations, knowing in your heart that they will be okay, and shifting your mind-set to focus on the positive will promote a much better experience for you both when you travel. Next time you travel, try these tips for an easier process.

1. Don't feel guilty about leaving them. There's no need to hide the suitcase and/or trick them to "protect" them. Be guilt-free and honest with them that you are leaving for a while and that they will be in good hands while you're away. This might mean verbally describing the trip or sending them mental images of the sun rising and setting the number of days you'll be gone.

2. If you are worried about your pet, they will sense it, which could cause them to feel unsafe. Believing in your heart that they are safe and attended to will assure them that this is in fact true and will help them become more independent. Before and during your

trip, send your animal companion mental images that they will have all of their needs taken care of and that they are good and are very loved.

3. While traveling, if you find your thoughts worrying about them, the best thing you can do for them is to gently shift your thoughts. Instead of worrying about them, send them love and a feeling of knowing that they are doing great. It's as simple as that. Just send them love. They will receive it. Even if they may have exhibited negative behaviors in the past while you are gone, sending them love instead of worry will help you both feel better.

These three steps can help with every life change they are going through.

Cultivate a Positive Mind-set with Rescue Animals

When I first began working with animals, I was shown through the gift of sensing energy the trauma or abuse the rescued animal had experienced, which could be affecting its behavior or showing up as illness. At times, it was horrendous to see what the animal had endured prior to their manifesting a better environment. Frequently animals take the brunt of having to deal with people who are unaware that the animals have souls, feelings, and emotional pain.

When I would share the images from their past with their caretakers, I often sensed these people instantly zero in on the trauma and what the animal had gone through despite their current, improved environment. Frequently they would imagine what the animal felt and begin relating to it to a point where it caused the person emotional pain to even look at the animal, which could delay or even stall the animal's healing process. It didn't take me long to make the decision to stop sharing the visuals because it did not serve a positive purpose for the animal or its caretakers.

It's common for animal-shelter volunteers and even new animal guardians to focus on and tell the animal's heartbreaking story, but it does not serve the animal for peoples' thoughts to be on what happened to them in the past. Animals are masters at being in the present moment and are here to teach us how to do the same. They are not as attached to their stories as people are and have innate survival abilities that allow them to move trauma out of their bodies and souls more so than people can. In the wild, animals are in life-or-death situations frequently. After the trauma is over and they are safe, they will tremble, twitch, shake, and even jump around to immediately discharge the energy of the event. Your animal companion has this same innate ability to discharge the energy from any past traumas as well.

> *Animals are masters at being in the*
> *present moment and are here to teach us*
> *how to do the same.*

Your animals are typically ready to move forward, heal, and begin anew. They manifested being saved, so they're already in alignment with a greater good and better outcome.

While I understand logically that knowing what an animal went through can help to put together the pieces of their story to better understand and treat their behavioral and/or physical issues, I learned that people naturally tend to focus on the abuse and can get stuck with that floating in their thoughts. This, in turn, can cause overnurturing (although with good intentions) to the point where an unhealthy codependent relationship is created.

Many years ago, Our Pal's Place in Marietta, Georgia, one of my favorite no-kill animal organizations, put together a team called Positive Energy and Thoughts (PET). Its purpose? Members collectively focus positive thoughts on a particular animal at the same time each evening. There is more power when a collective group is focusing on a positive outcome at the same time. Here's an example that derived from the PET teams' practice.

The Story of
Haley and Bennie

Haley, one of Our Pal's Place's rescue dogs, had a history of aggressive behavior toward Bennie, a much smaller, sweet-natured dog. They were not allowed to be in the same room together. I conducted a healing session on Haley, and, every evening thereafter, the PET team also visualized her feeling peaceful and calm with Bennie and the other dogs on-site. They also visualized her knowing and feeling that she was good (to help heal her core belief: "I'm bad").

Much to the staff's surprise, one day when a new volunteer accidentally allowed Haley to escape into the room where Bennie was, she ran right past him for the first time ever, and instead went straight to a person for attention. This was the first time that Haley never even looked at Bennie nor went after him full throttle. She ended up being adopted into a home that already had another dog, and they get along very peacefully.

Essential Wisdom

It's a gift to your rescue pets to focus on what you love about them, help them seek healing for their past, and provide a safe, patient home for their hearts to expand so they can continue serving the people in their lives. If you are open to more, know that they came into your life so that you can heal together. They will show you the way.

An Animal Visualization Meditation

During meditation we are better able to create the outcome we desire. The first step is to clear yourself and get connected. You might want to light a candle and find a comfortable place to sit quietly, uninterrupted.

Take a deep breath in and slowly exhale . . . take another breath in . . . exhale. Sitting comfortably now, and with every breath relaxing, relaxing, sense a golden light of protection and safety around you as you breathe.

Visualize white light flowing into the top of your head from the heart of heaven. Feel this pure connection of light flowing through you—it's of the highest vibration imaginable. Focus on the breath. In . . . out . . . Take a deep breath in . . . slowly exhale. This high vibrational light is slowly moving down the rest of your body and into the core of Mother Earth.

Breathe into this connection from heaven and Mother Earth. Feel and sense and relax into this divine connection. Feel the grace. Feel the strength. Feel the love.

Breathe into your heart . . . love . . . love . . . knowing and feeling that you are loved, that you *are* love . . . breathe this into your heart. Feel it.

(At this point, you might want to put a hand on your heart for comfort.)

You being here has made a positive difference for so many souls. You have contributed to raising Mother Earth's vibration of peace and love for all beings. Your presence is important to the Earth's balance.

Visualize yourself feeling loved and nurtured. Visualize there being enough love for you . . . filling you with divine love and light. There is enough. There has always been enough love for you. You are worthy and deserving of feeling this love that has arrived just for you.

Now bring your focus to the animals as a whole, and with the power of your mind, imagine all animals being respected, loved, and treated with compassion. See and know this to be true for all animals, plants, oceans, and people living as one harmoniously. Visualize this as you sit in the silence.

Imagine the Earth's vibration in complete harmony, with the prominent vibration being one of peace . . . one of love . . .

Feel the love that is flowing through you now.

Visualize animals living their lives in alignment and fulfilling their souls' purposes. Imagine them all feeling loved, nurtured, and having all of their needs met.

As you visualize the highest and best for each animal, you are also healing anything within you that might be in pain or feeling neglected, abandoned, or victimized.

Give yourself permission to let this beautiful golden light gently go to these areas within you for a peaceful and easy release.

Be gentle with yourself and know that you are always loved.

As you begin to come back to this present place and time, remember this feeling of harmony within and breathe in love and compassion for yourself and the animals as often as possible. You are worthy. You are important. You are love.

⁓⑨⑨⁓

13

Reaping the Rewards

Pssst . . . This is my favorite chapter of this book. If you read no other chapter in this book, it's my wish that you read this one chapter thoroughly. For if you're open to raising your awareness and looking under the cloaks of your emotional armoring, this chapter may be life-changing for you and your animals.

Truth: Our animals sense and pick up on our emotions. They can and will frequently absorb our energy—aka our emotional stuff. And if you're like me, that's the last thing you want for your beloved companions. Therefore, it's a gift to you both when you begin cracking the door to *your* emotional wounds and begin a personal journey of inner healing.

Most people don't go down that road because they don't know where to begin. And when it comes to healing their emotional wounds . . . well, people are pros at protecting their hearts and will unconsciously avoid "going there." If you're in animal rescue work or have guilt written into your family DNA, you might feel guilty spending time, money, or resources on yourself instead of others.

Do It for Them,
as Well as Yourself

When I realized just how much emotional baggage my animals were carrying for me, they became one of the biggest motivations for me to begin my own inner healing journey. They were frequently sick, and I spent a lot of time, focus, and funds tending to their physical issues. At the time, I had no idea what was really happening at an energetic level, but I observed and wondered why my animals seemed to have more physical issues than other people's pets did.

Ever since I began working on healing *me*, my animals have lived longer and have manifested fewer physical issues and negative behaviors. In addition, I went from having animals that didn't get along well together to ones who enjoy each other's companionship. Their interaction is always mirroring what is happening inside of us at some level. Working on our own inner healing is actually one of the fastest ways—if not the fastest way—to help the animals in our lives heal faster as well.

> *Working on our own inner healing is actually one of the fastest ways—if not the fastest way—to help the animals in our lives suffer less and heal faster.*

Know also that at a soul level, your companions willingly want to help you heal. Indeed, they came here and chose you specifically so they can evolve. There's no need to feel bad if you realize or fear they've picked up some of your repressed emotions. It's inevitable this will happen in any close relationship.

It might be easier than you think to begin taking steps

toward allowing more love, peace, joy, and well-being into your life. You might currently be putting yourself at the bottom of the list and have justified a busy life as the culprit, which is normal for most people. That's also called *resistance.*

When you embark on an intentional inner-healing journey, its value will expand through your life to all you love, including your animals, friends, and family. All of your relationships will be enhanced, or you will have discernment and the courage to end them if they are not meant to be part of your new path.

You are worthy and deserve the same amount of love and care that you give to your animal companions. It does not serve you at all to care for others and not yourself. Are you ready to feel better? Love more deeply? Feel love in your heart that you didn't know was possible? And—here's the biggest perk, animal lovers—are you ready to begin to feel safe and allow people to get as close to you as your animal companions do?

Finding the Right Energy Healer is Key

When I began my inner healing journey, I found I needed a healing practitioner to help me reach those places inside of myself where I'd never been before. At the time, I was suffering from many different physical ailments. As a result, I was on eight different daily medications I thought I'd be on for life and had a slew of surgeries under my belt, all of this healed in a matter of one or two years following my embracing of my deep healing journey.

Yes, it was worth it to feel so much better than I'd ever

felt before. I had many physical manifestations to begin with because I was a professional at pushing down my emotions, as many people are. The energy had no choice but to show up physically because I didn't have the inner resources in place to instead release my repressed emotions.

When I first embarked on my healing journey, I began to search for and met a handful or so of alternative holistic healers and psychotherapists. After a couple of months, with consistent focus, I found a qualified practitioner whom I trusted and with whom I felt safe. She also walked her talk and had a lot of integrity, both of which were very important to me.

I highly recommend finding **a certified energy healer** who trained under a teacher known for his or her integrity and credibility (my certification process took more than four years). Healing through the subtle energy field is an expedited healing process that most people naturally respond very positively to, more so than traditional talk therapy. Be that as it may, some people find the greatest efficacy comes from working with both types of therapy simultaneously.

Some signs you might need some help releasing energy and healing your emotional wounds are if you have physical manifestations and/or you are feeling sad, angry, insecure, depressed, anxious, or stressed out. Stress can really show up in the body, so it makes sense to have healthy habits in place and go-to options in your well-being tool bag for when life serves you experiences that trip you up.

Tips for a More Enhanced Outcome

Many people in my current client base began receiving sessions for themselves after observing their animals being calmer and more peaceful after their healing treatments. I would advise against using a friend to help you clear your deeper emotional wounds using energy healing, as it will probably result in a much lighter session. Although this can be a wonderful way to help you release the day's stress and get grounded, you could feel unsafe revealing all parts of yourself and any wounding that might come up for healing to a friend. It might also be very difficult for your friend to stay detached and offer unbiased guidance and feedback to you.

Keep your friends as friends, and use your healer only for healing. Blurring the boundaries here prevents the deeper work from revealing itself and could negatively affect a beautiful friendship. You will be led to the right practitioner and you will know when you have found the right person. Ask the universe, God, or your angels (two- and four-legged) to help you find the healing practitioner who is right for you, and trust your reaction to them. It's crucial that your healer is someone who can hold a space of heart-centered service to partner with you on your self-initiated healing journey. You'll know if their ego is in charge because they will need to be right and believe they have to have all the answers.

There are many modalities that can help you feel better. Most important is that you take a step forward and make a commitment to doing what you can to feel better so that you may show up in the world, shining your inner light. This I know for sure: you must try to release your resistance and avoidance so you can tap into the courage necessary to begin loving and taking care of yourself like never before. You are worth the effort. Really knowing this is key to allowing in a richer life experience. The act of self-love is the most powerful source of healing that there is.

There are many different paths and resources to support

your healing journey. At the minimum, I highly recommend developing a meditation practice. I have found—with myself, friends, and clients—how beneficial a meditation practice can be for one's well-being. And it's free! Meditating is easier than you might think, and it's gone mainstream. As a result, there are endless sources of information available to you, to help you set up a practice of your own. Books, guided meditation, and streaming meditation groups are plentiful and easy to find. Yoga, qigong, and t'ai chi are also great ways to move and balance your energy and to become connected. There are so many alternative modalities available, it can feel overwhelming, but just trust your gut and follow your inner guidance system. No one knows you like you!

For daily health and well-being, remember the acronym MEW, which stands for meditation, exercise (daily movement), and (plenty of) water. If you make these three pillars part of everyday life, you will go a long way toward curing "the daily crazies" and you will develop a positive core within. Make a commitment, on behalf of your animals, to lovingly care for yourself each and every day.

There are endless gifts that naturally arrive when you begin looking at your animals as messengers and guides. You will have a richer, more meaningful relationship that is not lined with misunderstanding or a fear of losing them and their love. As you become more aware and in sync with your animals, you will begin harvesting the extraordinary, intangible gifts that are the hidden keys to having healthy, loving relationships with them.

There are endless gifts that naturally arrive
when you begin looking at your animals
as messengers and guides.

Authenticity

There is hardly any greater gift you can give a person or an animal or any greater freedom you can feel than being able to be authentic in their presence. Once you are truthful in your expression of who you really are and what you really want, the relationship becomes more authentic, and you will both feel more comfortable, safe, and free to be real.

How might this apply to your animal? For example, if you've been sending your animal anger about a negative behavior of theirs, you might just be sending a superficial message. More likely than not, your anger is misdirected and is about something else altogether. When you can focus on your animal's inner light and tell them what you're wanting instead of what you don't want, they'll be able to hear your message, and the energy will be cleaner between the two of you.

It's important to be honest and authentic with them about what is happening in the house in regards to any big changes or moves, and even when you'll be traveling. They will appreciate your authenticity and honesty rather than being afraid of what you might *not* be telling them.

Look past your emotional triggers and see them for the loving beings they are at their core. When you can do this, they will more easily reflect that back to you.

Vulnerability

Being vulnerable means being willing to love unconditionally, even at the risk of having your heart broken. The word *vulnerability* actually comes from the Latin word for "wound," so it makes perfect sense that you would want to unconsciously protect your heart at all costs and resist being vulnerable. But if your psyche is set on autopilot to protect you from being hurt, for instance from losing a beloved animal, you will unconsciously create more detached relationships wherein you do not love with your whole heart. Alternately, you could be creating fear-based overloving relationships with your animals to avoid being vulnerable. Protecting your animal at every turn mirrors how you may be overprotecting your own heart as well.

Tell your inner child that she or he is safe to love and that any pain that might arise will not be too much to bear. The rewards of being vulnerable are worth it, for you will be able to feel more love and thus be able to open your heart so that love becomes the cornerstone of your relationship with your animals.

Peace

When you're able to receive your animals' messages, you will feel more peaceful. It really is that simple. Look for the gifts in their symbolic messages and in their mirroring. When you can understand the motivation behind their actions and your reactions to their behaviors, you will be able to return to a state of peaceful equilibrium more quickly.

Without realizing there is a higher purpose and plan for your relationship with your animals, you could be living on Crazy-Fix-It-Island, trying to fix their behavior or physical ailment one herb, medicine, or practitioner at a time. Once you observe the situation from a higher perspective, the sooner peace will arrive for you both.

Acceptance

There's so much power waiting for you when you accept your animals where they are emotionally, physically, and spiritually.

For in that moment in time, you will be holding up a mirror of acceptance for yourself. Their actions and behaviors are happening for a reason, and they will be more receptive to healing and change when you can accept them as they are first, and trust that they're moving forward at just the right and perfect pace for them.

Getting overly focused on wanting to change them actually keeps you both stuck. Sit back, relax, breathe, and accept that where you both are is all right. Releasing the stress for even a minute will help you have clarity, compassion, and acceptance with whatever issue is coming up for you and your animal companions.

Empowerment

Beginning to trust yourself to make the right decisions on behalf of your animals is very empowering. Believe in the fact that they are your decision-making partners and can give you signals, signs, and messages that pertain to what is in their highest and best interests.

It can be more difficult to feel confident with your decision-making abilities if you are in the middle of a difficult situation with your animals. Intentionally tapping into your adult, observer self in moments of crisis and following your heart is key to developing a more intimate and understanding relationship between you and your animals. You've got this!

Compassion

Finding compassion for your animals also reflects the degree to which you are able to have compassion for yourself. Having heartfelt compassion no matter what they are going through is a welcome gift to your relationship. For instance, it may be difficult if you've arrived home and notice that while you were out they've expressed themselves in a way you would prefer they hadn't. Look inside yourself and find compassion for them. From that place, divine answers are birthed. Undoubtedly a kinder, better solution to help them will emerge.

Maybe you've been working with a very scared animal and have been patient and kind, but it has been a difficult experience nonetheless. Finding compassion for yourself in the midst of challenging times with your animals can promote healthy crying. Tears are filled with the divine release of your pain. I highly recommend that you give yourself permission to cry as needed. You and your animals will both benefit when you release your pain rather than repressing it and covering it up.

A Higher Level of Consciousness

Once you build the muscle of tuning in to your animals and receiving their real messages, you will perceive that more frequently, they are providing answers to your questions—not only about them, but about other issues in your life as well. Remember how my cat Sundance showed me I was repressing anger for doing work that I no longer loved by sitting on my desk and meowing when I was on conference calls? Or how MaiTai found a way to jump on top of the armoire and showed me there was another option to a problem I had? Through the incredible experience of connecting with your companions in a new expanded way, you will also start sensing the overall interconnectedness of all beings in the universe.

You might observe yourself feeling safer because you know instinctively that you are never alone and that you'll be okay no matter what. Raising your consciousness around your animals and having deeper insights as to why they are in your life will be life-changing for you both.

Well-Being

Understanding your animals' needs and desires will bring well-being and health to you and to your animal companions. If you also choose to be kinder to yourself and take responsibility for your own inner healing, the well-being and health of your body, mind, and soul will also be enhanced. This may manifest as instantaneous healing in some aspect of your life, or a slow and steady healing progression of some other issue over time. However it shows up, you'll definitely notice a positive change for the better in terms of your long-term wellness, which will also be reflected in your relationships with your animal companions.

An Enhanced Spiritual Connection

Raising your awareness around this beautiful relationship you have with your animal and noticing the positive changes in you both will arrive with the feeling of knowing that you are connected to God, to Mother Earth, and to all there is. Through meditation and intention, you will begin to open yourself to that wonderful feeling of spiritual bliss. Believing in a higher power, God, or an intelligent source of good in the universe will greatly enhance your ability to allow in all of the other gifts listed in this chapter.

Sit for a few minutes every day in stillness. Perhaps put your hand on your heart, and express heartfelt gratitude for something in your life, however small, and feel the opening of love in your heart. This feeling is capturing the divine love that is in and around you all the time, every moment of the day. The more you tap into this feeling, the easier every single aspect of your life and relationships will be.

Your animals already know how to feel this, however, your intentional tuning into it will help them immensely. *The better you feel, the better they feel.*

Essential Wisdom

It is difficult for me to find the words to express how much better you can feel and how much richer your life can be when you find the courage within to undertake a deep, emotional healing journey. It is beyond life-changing. It is the marriage of grace and gratitude by your inner love doctor. This feeling extends not only to yourself, but to all the beings who you love.

Love is not treats or toys or an expensive bed. But you already know that, right? It's also not expecting your animal companions to act a certain way to please you or giving you adoration no matter how you treat them. Love is when you and your animals come together with big open hearts that are already full of love—self-love *and* divine love. At this point the overflow of love, from the hearts of both of you, meets and is shared in a gift that just keeps on giving.

Love is being in the present moment to see and connect with them. Love is honoring them by being awake to their teachings. Real love is letting them love you back because you see yourself as lovable too.

You are in each other's lives to expand the love in your hearts. Let love always be your guide.

Love recognizes no barriers. It jumps hurdles, leaps fences, penetrates walls to arrive at its destination, full of hope.

MAYA ANGELOU

EPILOGUE

Their Love Letter to You

Over the years, I've seen and felt consistent messages flow from the animals I've loved and the thousands of animals I've been honored to work with that, when embraced by their humans as truth, have made a positive, life-changing difference in both of their lives. If your animal could write you a love letter, I think it would look something like this:

To My Beloved Person,

My heart is full of gratitude to you for creating a safe place for me to live, love, heal, and enjoy life. Thank you for being open to healing together. If you find yourself stuck in fear because of an issue that you perceive I'm going through or an emotion that you assume I must be feeling, pull back your energy and release your fears in healthy ways. Then you will have clarity about what matters most to us both.

During stressful times, I understand that you are doing the best you can, so please, release any guilt that you are hanging onto regarding decisions on my behalf. I forgive you for any perceived mistakes. Let's move forward and not look back at unpleasant times. Focusing on the past keeps us both stuck.

Speak your truth to me. I can handle it. When you're leaving the house for whatever reason, believe that I will be fine, as that helps me release my own fears. Send me love when you're not with me. I will feel it, and it helps me to feel more peaceful and safe when you are not physically with me.

Please honor any grieving process I may be going through and give me the space and timing to heal as I choose. Feel free to grieve with me and know that releasing my pain during difficult times is a natural thing that I need to do. I know it hurts you to see me hurting but know that I'll be okay, just as you will.

Love yourself as much as I love you. Look in the mirror and see what I see: a beautiful, kind, loving, caring person filled with light and love. It has and always will be easy for me to see that you are a spark of the Divine. When I see you being kinder to yourself, I have accomplished one of my goals, and that helps my soul to evolve.

What you feed me matters. A lot. Please give me higher-vibrational food to help me better take care of my sacred temple and help me not to confuse food with love. Also feed me positive, loving thoughts grounded with a knowing that everything is always unfolding just as it should be.

I need daily movement to release my emotions and feel better. It helps me to ground with Mother Earth, and it revitalizes my body, mind, and soul. It also clears toxins and energy I might have absorbed from others.

My soul is evolving, and being with you is important for my growth. I know you think you chose me, but I always knew you were the one for me. The heavens orchestrated every detail to ensure that we'd be together, however short our time might be. Together we can be a bridge from heaven to earth and bring more light to this world.

I am not the reason you feel more love; you were simply ready to begin opening your heart, and God sent me to you. I cannot love you enough to heal your pain. That is yours to bear, heal, and release on your own. However, know that I will always support you by loving you, no matter what you may be going through, and I will hold space for you to find the strength and courage you need to begin removing the cloaks of your pain so you may feel better. I will be your number one cheerleader.

When it is my time to go, know that I will help you with any big decisions you have to make on my behalf. I trust you completely to accurately read my wishes. I do not fear death, as I know I will always be around you, just in a different way.

Be a role model for love. When you are able to quiet your inner critic and begin to shift how you treat yourself, you allow more love to enter your heart. And when you allow in more love, you have more love to give. And that is why we are both here.

With great respect, love, and gratitude,
Your Animal Companion

∗

In memory of my beloved MaiTai
2000–2018

Resources

General Resources

Healing Touch for Animals® provides a multilevel curriculum courses designed for all animal lovers looking to improve the lives of their animals through hands-on energy therapy.
healingtouchforanimals.com

Reading Paws is a nationwide program hosted at schools and libraries. Volunteer teams of dogs and caregivers connect with children to help them learn to love reading.
readingpaws.org

Silvia Hartmann's Energy Healing for Animals certification course teaches a student to do energy healing on any animal and includes information about how to build a business.
dragonrising.com/store/distance_learning/
energy_healing_for_animals/

Recommended Reading

Animal-Speak and *Animal-Wise* by Ted Andrews
Created to help you understand the symbolic gifts and

messages from animals that show up in your life, this book also provides guidance to help interpret what your animals are trying to tell you.

Light Emerging by Barbara Ann Brennan
Prior to acquiring my Interface Therapy Certification, this book was my go-to in my healing practice. Discover in-depth research into the energy exchange between people, as well as the core emotional wounds all people are here to heal.

Meditation for the Love of It by Sally Kempton
This is my favorite book on meditation. Sally offers many different styles and techniques for meditation that promote an open-minded acceptance of yourself and whatever level of meditation you may practice.

Owning Your Own Shadow by Robert A. Johnson
This small but powerful book will help you understand the beauty in your shadow.

Saying Good-Bye to the Pet You Love
by Lorri A. Greene, Ph.D., and Jacquelyn Landis
Beautifully written, this book will lovingly guide you through the process of your pet's final chapter.

The Subtle Body: An Encyclopedia of Your Energetic Anatomy by Cyndi Dale
This extraordinary book examines energy maps of the body from around the world, from ancient times to presentday.

Lift and Shift Books You'll Love
Living Beautifully with Uncertainty and Change
by Pema Chodron

Return to Love by Marianna Williamson

Seven Spiritual Laws of Success by Deepak Chopra

The Four Agreements
by Don Miguel Ruiz and Janet Mills

The Seat of the Soul by Gary Zukav

The Untethered Soul by Michael A. Singer

Whatever Arises, Love That by Matt Kahn

Lift and Shift Books about Animals
Learning Their Language by Marta Williams

The Art of Racing in the Rain by Garth Stein

The Divinity of Dogs by Jennifer Skiff

*The Ten Trusts: What We Must Do to Care for
the Animals We Love* by Jane Goodall and Marc Bekoff

When Elephants Weep: The Emotional Lives of Animals
by Jeffrey Moussaieff Masson and Susan McCarthy

Finding Help
through Bioenergetic Healing

There are many certification paths to become a practitioner in the field of energy healing. If you are considering working with a professional energy healer, it is important to know your healer is coming from a place of integrity and you believe that they are partnering *with* you on your healing journey versus telling you what to do. Ultimately, your healing will be long-lasting when you trust and believe in yourself more than anyone else. Keep your power with whatever healer you choose.

Tips for Identifying the Best Energy Healer for You and/or Your Animals

1. Ask them about their background, training certifications and how long they have been in practice.

2. Look at their online presence and read the testimonials. Do you resonate with and like what you see?

3. Your sessions will be much more productive if the healer has a clear connection to spirit and is as healthy as possible. Alcohol, drugs/medications, and even unhealthy eating habits can negatively affect the healer's effectiveness. You'll get a sense of their energy when with them.

4. Trust your gut. Do they feel like someone you can trust with your well-being? With your pets'? Do you feel comfortable and safe in their presence to reveal even the parts of yourself that you judge? That's what is needed for you to begin a deeper healing journey and to truly begin releasing your inner core emotional wounds.

5. Inquire if they also work with a healer to get cleared and/or mentored. Have they themselves embarked on an inner healing journey to clear their energy and emotional wounds?

6. Do they walk their talk? If the answer is yes, they are likely living and working in integrity and qualified to help you or your pet heal.

7. Commit to the healer and your inner healing journey. Once you find someone you like and trust it is a gift to your soul to find the courage to commit to the beautiful unfolding of your healing journey.

Additional Work by Me

My semimonthly column "Animals as Guides," which can be read in past issues of *Conscious Life Journal,* educates people to better interpret animals and help them feel better. Each issue also highlights an animal rescue organization.

Visit the journal's website:
https://myconsciouslifejournal.com

I am a co-author of *F.A.I.T.H.: Finding Answers in the Heart*, an inspirational and encouraging book written by courageous women of spirit who share their stories of struggle and triumph.

Visit the book's website:
findinganswersintheheart.com

My self-help CD, *Embracing the Divine Within: Meditations for a Loving, Thriving Life,* is heart centered and deeply healing, and includes three powerful meditations to help you relax and release, with the intent of feeling more peaceful and allowing more abundance and love into your life.

http://tammybillups.com/embracing-divine-within

Connect with Me

Website—**tammybillups.com**
Blog—**tammybillups.com/blog**
Facebook pages—**fb/soulhealingwithouranimalcompanions**
or **fb/sundancehealing**
Instagram—**tammybillups1122**
Linked In—**www.linkedin.com/in/tammy-billups-8373568**

Rescue an Animal ~ Open Your Heart

Are you looking for a new animal to join your family? So many orphaned animals in the world need loving forever homes. The fine organizations listed below were highly recommended by the supporters of this book because they had a positive experience with them. You might want to contact one of these animal organizations to see if your next four-legged family member is waiting for you there.

Angels Among Us
angelsrescue.org

Atlanta Humane Society
atlantahumane.org

Best Friends Animal Society
bestfriends.org

Brother Wolf Animal Rescue
bwar.org

Cavaschon Shelter,
East Coast Humane Society
eastcoasthumanesociety.com

Cherokee County Animal Shelter
cherokeega-animals.org

Feline Rescue, Inc.
felinerescue.org

Furkids
furkids.org

Georgia Jack Russell
Rescue Sanctuary
jackrusselladoptions.org

Georgia Poodle Rescue
georgiapoodlerescue.com

Good Mews
goodmews.org

Mostly Mutts Animal Shelter
mostlymutts.org

Our Pal's Place
ourpalsplace.org

PAWS
paws.org

Paws Atlanta
pawsatlanta.org

Planned Pethood
pethoodga.org

Rabun Paws 4 Life
rabunpaws4life.com

Rat Terrier Rescue
newrattitude.org

Rescue Ranch Pups, Inc.
rescueranchpups.org

Save the Horses
savethehorses.org

Small Dog Rescue
smalldogrescue.com

About the Author

At the turn of the millennium, Tammy was the epitome of the American success story—a top biller and senior partner at a national recruiting firm. But the death of her mother in 1999 was quickly followed by the passing of all three of her beloved animal companions and the sudden recall of horrendous childhood memories. All of this trauma prompted Tammy's spiritual awakening and inner healing journey.

In the midst of it all Tammy's now widely celebrated energetic healing abilities and intuitive gifts emerged. After receiving her first bioenergetic healing session, which produced immediate results, Tammy spontaneously realized her life's purpose.

Today, after facilitating thousands of healing sessions with people and animals nationwide and numerous appearances on TV, radio, and podcasts—including CNN's *The Daily Share*, *Primetime Live ABC*, and *The Oprah Winfrey Show*—Tammy is excited to share her knowledge and the wisdom she has garnered about the deeper connection that exists between people and their animal companions.

Tammy is certified in Interface Therapy through the Center for Integrative Therapy and is an animal energy healer.

She founded the animal ministry at the Southeast's largest Unity Spiritual Center in 2004 and currently facilitates its monthly Praying Paws Animal Service. In addition to donating weekly sessions to animal-rescue centers, she also penned a column called "Animals as Guides" for *Conscious Life Journal* and continues to serve on its editorial board. Tammy is the coauthor of the inspirational book *F.A.I.T.H.: Finding Answers in the Heart,* and in 2014 she released the self-help CD *Embracing the Divine Within: Meditations For a Loving, Thriving Life.* Together with her cat companions, Sundance and MaiTai, Tammy makes her home in a suburb of Atlanta, Georgia.

For more information about Tammy, please visit tammybillups .com or facebook.com/soulhealingwithouranimalcompanions.

Index

Books of Related Interest

Animal Voices, Animal Guides
Discover Your Deeper Self through Communication with Animals
by Dawn Baumann Brunke

Shapeshifting with Our Animal Companions
Connecting with the Spiritual Awareness of All Life
by Dawn Baumann Brunke

Animal Messengers
An A-Z Guide to Signs and Omens in the Natural World
by Regula Meyer

Speaking with Nature
Awakening to the Deep Wisdom of the Earth
by Sandra Ingerman and Llyn Roberts

Psychic Communication with Animals for Health and Healing
by Laila del Monte

White Spirit Animals
Prophets of Change
by J. Zohara Meyerhoff Hieronimus, D.H.L.

Becoming Nature
Learning the Language of Wild Animals and Plants
by Tamarack Song

How Animals Talk
And Other Pleasant Studies of Birds and Beasts
by William J. Long

INNER TRADITIONS • BEAR & COMPANY
P.O. Box 388
Rochester, VT 05767
1-800-246-8648
www.InnerTraditions.com

Or contact your local bookseller